"Interesting?"

With love from Gran
"A merry Christmas"

Worse Things Happen At Sea

Worse Things Happen At Sea

compiled and edited by

COMMANDER E. F. PRITCHARD RN
and
RICHARD BLADON

ABSON BOOKS · ABSON · WICK · BRISTOL

Acknowledgements

The Trustees of the National Lifeboat Museum
wish to express their thanks to the following publishers
for permission to use extracts from books
originally published by them:

Hodder & Stoughton Ltd. *A Touch of the Memoirs*
by Donald Sinden and *The Eye of the Wind* by Sir Peter Scott.

Arrow Books *I Search for Rainbows* by Barbara Cartland.

Hutchinson Publishing Group *At One with the Sea*
by Dame Naomi James.

First published in Great Britain in 1983
by ABSON BOOKS, Abson, Wick, Bristol

Copyright © The National Lifeboat Museum, Bristol, 1983
Copyright © Drawings – Peter J. Stuckey
All royalties to The National Lifeboat Museum

ISBN 0 902920 54 5

Printed at the Burleigh Press, Bristol England

Contents

FOREWORD
HRH Prince Philip

BUCKINGHAM PALACE.

It is impossible to eliminate the chance of accidents in any human activity. If that activity takes place in such an unstable medium as the sea, the chances of an accident are that much greater, the consequences that much more serious and the rescue of lives in danger that much more difficult. If there is any doubt about this, even a casual glance through the stories in this book should be enough to dispel it.

Strange and wonderful things happen at sea, but I can imagine nothing more wonderful than the sight of an approaching life-boat when all hope of survival seems to have gone.

The proceeds of this book go to the National Life-Boat Museum, itself a memorial and tribute to the generations of volunteer lifeboatmen who have gone to the help of those in peril on the sea.

1983

Preface

We are indebted to His Royal Highness The Prince Philip, Duke of Edinburgh for his foreword to this volume and to all the contributors, without exception extremely busy people, who have readily given time and trouble to write to us with their own particular tales of the sea.

All the profits from this book are going towards the completion of the National Lifeboat Museum, which is already partially open in the City Docks in the heart of Bristol. The project began more than six years ago when a group of lifeboat enthusiasts, headed by Mr Peter Elliott, suddenly realised that, with the coming of new types of boats made in modern synthetic materials, the old hand-crafted wooden lifeboats would soon disappear completely. With the support of the RNLI and Bristol City Council, a fine collection of lifeboats, some dating from the days of sail, has been built up in a converted dockside warehouse. The older boats are being lovingly restored, the collection is constantly growing and summer by summer is attracting larger numbers of visitors. Once the Museum has been completed, all proceeds will go direct to the RNLI for the benefit of Britain's volunteer lifeboat service, which is the envy of the world.

The editors would like to pay special tribute to Mr Graham Penticost, the Maritime Bristol Co-ordinator, for his advice and practical help, also to Sue Sheppard – The No. 1 Staff Bureau, Bristol – for preparing the manuscript for publication free of charge, and to all the other people who have turned what once seemed a hare-brained idea into a practical fund-raising project.

E.F.P.
R.B.

Lord Cudlipp

FORMER CHAIRMAN,
INTERNATIONAL PUBLISHING CORPORATION

I have never complained about it in a churlish manner, but I have felt for many years aggrieved that my uncanny skill as an Emergency Instant Navigator of small ships in the English Channel and beyond has been insufficiently recognised. I welcome the publication of *Worse Things Happen at Sea* as an opportunity to mention in passing, three incidents for the record: not in the expectation of any special award from Prince Philip – a sea-green plaque in the National Lifeboat Museum will suffice.

It was always a crew of friends, one of whom was a brilliant navigator. I always kept a wary eye on the shipping forecast, that's for sure, but was usually too busy being captain and bartender to worry about the nitty-gritty like courses, fog and E.T.A. I believed in delegation, and my reputation as a master mariner was solely based upon extra-sensory perception and my cool performance in moments of crisis.

Case I: Any fool, with exceptions, can cross from Dover to Calais, but it is possible to miss the target, which we did. It didn't occur to anybody on board to seek the captain's opinion until we were bobbing around near a crowd of Frenchmen paddling on a beach. I instantly knew they were French because I could detect their accent: it was France, but it wasn't Calais.

'No panic', I said. 'Cruise over to that fishing boat, get me the loud hailer, and leave the rest to me.'

'*Bon jour*', I bawled as we came alongside, '*où est Calais?*' And when the fishermen stopped laughing they pointed vigorously to the right (or west). I made no mention of the matter when we reached Calais an hour later.

1

Case II: Admittedly we had enjoyed a lavish pre-cruise dinner in Ramsgate, with brandy at the captain's expense, and admittedly it was pea-soup foggy. The destination was Ostend – easier to depart from, it appeared, than to arrive at. I was rather surprised to be awakened from my slumber during the all-night crossing to be told that 'we don't know where we are and we are an hour overdue'. Charts and pilot books were strewn around the cabin and the navigator confessed he was perplexed.

'No panic', I said. 'Hand me the binoculars'. Dimly, on that cold damp dawn, I perceived a long slab of concrete jutting out to the sea.

'We are about to disembark', I said calmly, 'at Zeebrugge.' The announcement was received by the navigator with a coarse word which, roughly translated, hinted that I was talking through my hat.

'Zeebrugge it is', I repeated, and it was. Years before I had read a book about the renowned raid on that German submarine base during World War I and I remembered the picture of The Mole, the massive 1½ mile breakwater which shields the harbour.

These two feats caused a certain amount of talk (principally from me), but my reputation as Emergency Instant Navigator was finally established (or at any rate in my own estimation) by what I occasionally call The Miracle of Boulogne. We were crossing from Dieppe to Dover, which sounds simple, but all hell broke loose that night with even our engines (petrol!) taking fright. Thunder storms and angry seas – the lot. Captain Ahab would have suffered a thrombosis in his ivory leg.

The navigator prudently suggested a starboard lurch to Boulogne, which would hopefully reduce the ordeal by three hours in my creaking wooden boat. He added ruefully, after another engine breakdown, 'God knows how we'll find it'.

'Gentlemen', I announced at the appropriate moment,

'we'll stay on course. We'll be in Boulogne in half-an-hour', dismissing the scepticism of the crew with a brief reference to '*Où est Calais*?' and The Mole.

'Well', said the navigator over the coffee and brandy in the all-night portside bar, 'it was bloody luck that time.'

'No, gentlemen', said the Emergency Instant Navigator. 'Not luck. During a flash of forked lightning I saw for one second the Colonne de la Grande Armée. . . .'

I could go on, but have no wish to delay the opening of the National Lifeboat Museum.

'Helen Blake' 1938–1957

Alistair Cooke KBE (Hon)

JOURNALIST AND BROADCASTER

Thirty-odd years ago, I was crossing on the *Queen Mary* from Southampton to New York. On the second day, I struck up an acquaintance with a dapper, middle-aged man who described himself as 'a retired writer'. He and an American friend who was also aboard formed a little syndicate to bet on 'the ship's pool', the nightly auction of the passengers' estimates of the next day's run. During the last full day of the ship's passage, the ship slowed to a crawl, on the suspicion that there was a man overboard. It turned out to be a false rumour. That night, our 'retired writer' lost a bet along with the syndicate but won the pool with the low number, on which he had placed a secret bet. When we berthed at New York, I asked him who could possibly have started such a gruesome rumour. He simply winked.

I was so excited by the dramatic possibilities of this event that I sat down and wrote a first draft of a screenplay. The following week, by sheer coincidence, the *New Yorker* magazine, published a chilling story by Roald Dahl on exactly the same theme, clinched, however, with the ingenious idea of having the winner actually push an old lady overboard. It was called as I recall, 'A Dip in the Pool'. My movie remained unwritten and unmade, but the memory of this cunning bit of bounderism has never faded.

Harry Carpenter

TELEVISION SPORTS BROADCASTER

I was in the RN during the war, working as a wireless telegraphist (I think they call them something else today: radio operator?)

Part of my time was spent in the Mediterranean, aboard a Hunt-class destroyer HMS *Whaddon*. I can remember being very seasick at times, but such minor ailments were no excuse to miss duty and so I sat at my Morse key with a bucket by my side. Recovering from one of these uncomfortable sessions, I lay in my hammock on the mess deck, queasily dozing when a disturbing noise brought me wide awake.

There was a scraping and a clanking, a metallic thumping, which somehow seemed to be coming from outside the ship. It lasted, I suppose, about 10 seconds and sounded for all the world as if someone OUTSIDE was knocking to come in. It stopped, and I fell asleep.

When I woke up, the mess deck was crowded. 'Didn't you hear the bumping going on?' someone asked.

'Yes, I did', I said. 'What was it?'

'We scraped a mine, but it didn't go off!'

Not much of a story, really, but it was as close to extinction as I've come.

Lord Rothermere

CHAIRMAN, ASSOCIATED NEWSPAPERS GROUP

It was one of those Mediterranean dawns that promised another glorious day, as it should towards the end of May. The wind was south-west, force 4, but the swell was heavier than it should have been – and perhaps that ought to have told us something.

By noon, Cape Vaticano was abeam and we shaped course for the Straits of Messina, bound for Reggio. We'd hit the south-going tide just right. The wind was still force 4, but the swell was, if anything, worse. Not that, in a 44 ft Hatteras cruiser with a twin 175 hp diesels, it worried us overmuch.

In fact, we were having coffee and talking of Charybdis and Scylla when we saw that the wind had backed to just west of south, and in a few moments had moved up to force 7.

Spray had begun to lift off the seas and we saw a fishing trawler steaming full belt towards us and on towards Cape Vaticano without so much as a glance. Perhaps that should have told us something too! The wind increased until we had to shout to be heard. We reduced speed again, but still we were reluctant to give up a favourable tide. With the wind up to force 8, we slammed on into head seas which towered above us and then buried our stem in a mass of water.

Suddenly, there was an almighty crack. The navigator and our skipper rushed below. A porthole in the forecastle had stove in. Gallons of water gushed in with every slam.

While the two below stuffed the hole with cushions and blankets, I put the boat over to take the seas on the other bow. As they worked below cutting up oars and bits of floor-boards to keep the stuffing in the porthole. I got the motor-pump started. Fortunately it worked!

We were not far from Scylla, marked on the chart, and we now had a 'Charybdis and Scylla' choice – to go on and risk another flooding in the rising seas – and no RNLI in sight – or risk broaching on the return journey and flooding that way.

After a few moments discussion, I decided to turn. We waited for a 'smooth' and pushed the boat round on the engines. We could hear water sloshing about in the bilge, in spite of the pump, for our temporary repair was anything but water-tight.

With the seas on our port quarter and Cape Vaticano to leeward on our starboard bow, we began the tricky passage back. The skipper worked the throttles against every broach and I did my best, in between, to inch the boat off shore. The navigator kept a wary eye on the land, between dashing below to attend to our 'repair'.

After a wet, anxious, noisy and viciously windy three hours, we crawled behind Cape Vaticano, and suddenly there was no wind at all. We dropped anchor in the first small harbour we came to. If it hadn't been for the sodden cushions and blankets and the squelching carpets we might never have believed it had happened to us as we sat with a reviving drink warmed by the afternoon sun and overlooked by the magnificent walled town of Tropea.

Admiral Sir Raymond Lygo KCB

MANAGING DIRECTOR, BRITISH AEROSPACE

All of us who have been fortunate enough to have command of one of Her Majesty's warships, from time to time, will be familiar with the routine at the Captain's table where the Captain, who is both judge and jury, exercises his powers of discipline as laid down in the Naval Discipline Act. Minor misdemeanours require a standard procedure which involves the charge being read, the accused being asked how he pleads; in the case of a plea of guilty a statement can be made in mitigation either of character or circumstance, usually presented by the divisional officer.

Every ship has its 'skate', and if it is unlucky, several 'skates'. Chaps who live just barely one side of the law – or not quite, and cause and generate a disproportionate amount of work and effort. It becomes a game between the Coxswain or the Master at Arms, depending on the size of the ship, and the Commander or First Lieutenant, to nail these malefactors as they are a constant source of irritation to the management, and of interest and amusement to the entire ship's company, if they manage to slip through the net once again.

On one such occasion, a rating who had been a fairly persistent late arriver on board was hauled up on this third repeated offence. He duly appeared at my table and was a subject of curiosity to the assembled officers. The charge read: 'That he did return on board HMS Blank, twenty minutes adrift on the certain date, this being a third repeated offence'. The lad pleaded guilty and I asked if he wished to make a statement in mitigation.

He said, 'Yes Sir, it is like this, my wife has a budgie'.

At this point, everybody was taking a much closer interest in the proceedings. I leaned forward, anxious to know the connection between the wife's budgie and the late return on board. He continued, 'She is very fond of it, Sir, and she keeps it in a cage and takes it everywhere with her and at night she brings it into the bedroom, Sir, and it sits in its cage on the side of the bed, Sir. Well, Sir, knowing I had to be on board at eight o'clock, I set my alarm for six so I should be up in plenty of time to be able to get back to my ship, as required, Sir.'

'Go on', I said.

'Well, Sir, in the middle of the night the budgie must have got out of his cage, Sir, and he must have flown around the room, Sir, and then, not knowing where he was, settled on top of the little knob of the alarm clock and held it down and as a result it didn't go off and I was late getting up, Sir and I was late returning back on board, Sir.'

I looked at him with interest. A true dispenser of justice requires a little humanity or sense of humour and sometimes a little more tolerance than perhaps the case deserves, but a good story deserves its own reward. 'Case dismissed', I said, to the intense annoyance of the First Lieutenant and the Coxswain.

Afterwards, as I said to them, 'No harm has really been done by this, it will be a good tonic for the ship's company and I am sure you will get him next time, and he won't be able to tell that story again – well not to this Captain anyway'.

Peter Alliss

GOLFER, SPORTS BROADCASTER AND WRITER

The Family Alliss, in the early days, were renowned sailors, indeed, my grandfather, Captain J. Rust, had two trawlers which plied their way from Hull out into the North Sea, then, in the latter part of his life, from Swansea out into the Atlantic and up into the Icelandic fishing areas, where he was one of the earliest discoverers of those massive shoals of fish. Grandad Rust had salt water coursing though his veins. At this moment, I am sitting looking at a very splendid picture of him in his Captain's uniform, very fine with that rather stern face and glorious walrus moustache.

Captain Rust was on my mother's side of the family, we Allisses, on the other hand, were landlubbers to say the least. My father once told me that in the '30s, when he was competing for Great Britain against the United States in the Ryder Cup, he was actually seasick whilst the great liner was tied up in dock at Southampton; this pedigree did not bode well for me. In fact, as I have grown older, I have been known to feel slightly queasy on a damp lawn.

I was a big boy, nothing to be afraid of, masses of advice – take the pills – look at the horizon, get in the middle of the ship, don't forget to be in the fresh air away from the diesel fumes. Well, several years ago my wife and I had a holiday in Greece, we had a week in Corfu and a week on the splendid island of Paxos. Paxos in those days was relatively undiscovered and slightly primitive, but what a magical place it was. Peter Bull, the well-known actor and collector of teddy bears, was the most famous resident and how often I used to watch him sitting in the little square on the edge of the quay, watching the fishing boats come in and drinking the local brew, which, if I remember rightly, tasted quite disgusting until you had got 7 or 8 down you, then it became quite pleasant. The holiday was a great success, then came time for our return.

The trip out had been like a mill pond; I had been a bit of a poseur going round the deck of the (to me) not-inconsiderably-sized ship, looking over the rail, looking wise, looking up, looking down, taking photos, and for all the world to see I was indeed a middle-aged mariner. I would tell them when I got home.

The return journey looked O.K. when we were in the harbour, we were loaded to the gunwales, chugged away waving to the friendly faces on the shore, out of the tiny harbour back to Corfu. We hadn't gone more than 500 yards, indeed out of the harbour and round the headland, when I noticed that there were one or two white horses beginning to appear on what in the harbour had looked like a mirror-like sea. The next 10 minutes saw a change in weather that you wouldn't believe. I will not say it was a gale force wind, but suddenly our boat, which I had thought was a miniature *Queen Mary* now looked more like one of those coracles that wander up and down the River Severn; hither and thither and up and down. The couple we were with were good sailors and my wife, well you could have waves 100 feet high and I don't think she would turn a hair.

They thought a bottle of beer would do me good. It didn't. Getting to the bar was an experience I will never forget, already one or two passsengers were looking queasy and there were those familiar, none-too-pleasant sounds people make when leaning far out over the rail. The only thing to do in the circumstances was to sit very quietly, which I did.

I was amazed at the Greek sailors, barefooted, about 5′ 5″, arms like tree trunks, trousers rolled up just beneath the knees, walking about without holding on to anything as the ship pitched and rolled and the moaning went on and my face went paler and paler. I must indeed have looked like Marley's Ghost. It took a couple of hours or so to reach port and I don't think I have felt such relief as the ship started to slow down and stop rocking and rolling about. We tied up at the quayside. My wife, bless her, had not said a word, she knew how I was feeling, took my hand and guided me ashore. Four deep breaths didn't help the cause much, I looked back; the sailors were busy tying up, getting the luggage off; for them it was just another routine journey, for me it was going to be my very last journey by sea.

'Never again' was the cry, but I have said that after a night on the Johnny Walker and not kept my promise. So look out sea, you haven't beaten me yet. But there again. . . .

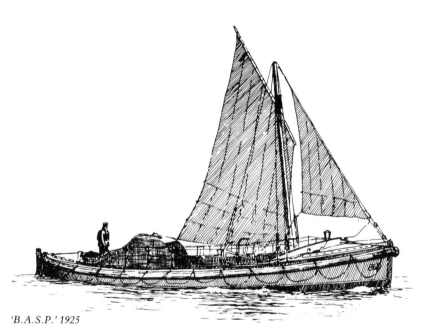

'B.A.S.P.' 1925

Sir Bernard Lovell OBE FRS

FORMER DIRECTOR, JODRELL BANK
EXPERIMENTAL STATION AND
EMERITUS PROFESSOR OF RADIO ASTRONOMY,
UNIVERSITY OF MANCHESTER

The boy was about 7 or 8 years old. He seemed minute beside the large man and I wondered how the small inflatable dinghy kept them afloat. It was early evening on the last day of July 1976 and I spotted them first when I rounded the East headland of our small island in Bantry Bay. Apart from the odd sight of the man and the boy in that dinghy, the bay was deserted.

I had taken our fishing boat out to catch a few mackerel for our island supper, but the dinghy was already far beyond the stretch of water beyond the two islands which was as far as I liked to venture when alone. I let down the feathers a couple of times and then noticed that the man was trying unsuccessfully to start the engine on the dinghy. Meanwhile the stiff off-shore breeze was carrying me too close to the rocks of Sheelane and the man and the boy were already South of this outer island with more than twenty fathoms of water beneath them.

I started my engine and got within hailing distance. Did he need help? 'No' was the reply, so I resumed my fishing. A few minutes more and it became evident that he did need help. Having failed to start the engine the man was attempting to row by using his hands and he and the boy were receding rapidly from land. Once more I wound up my line and this time got close enough to converse with him. He had neither paddles, nor life-jackets and had no idea what was wrong with the engine.

Then it was my turn to make a bad mistake. He and the boy refused to climb from the dinghy into my boat and, since we

13

were both drifting much further from land than I cared to be I eventually threw him a rope and hoped that my Seagull would stand the strain of towing a heavily-loaded dinghy to safety. It was too much to hope, but mercifully it did not fail until we were within rowing distance of our small landing stage.

My wife, who had been watching the scene through binoculars with increasing alarm, was there with a bottle of Paddy and chocolate for the boy. Only then did the full horror of the situation dawn. The boy was German and could not speak English. The man had no connection whatsoever with the boy. He had simply seen him on the mainland jetty and beckoned him into the dinghy. Furthermore, the man did not own the dinghy. He had borrowed it from another stranger on the jetty. The only trouble with their engine was that it had run out of petrol. They had neither a reserve, nor paddles, nor life-jackets on board!

Eventually I returned them to the mainland to be met by the young and irate mother of the boy. She was distraught because our island completely blocked from view the part of the sea where I had taken them in tow and in a torrent of German she began her abuse of the youngster. She might have had a word of thanks I mused as I returned to our island or, better still, have used her vocabulary to chastise the man for so stupidly endangering the life of her son.

Commander E F Pritchard RN

FUND-RAISING DIRECTOR, NATIONAL
LIFE-BOAT MUSEUM

Returning one day to Istanbul from Principo in the Sea of
Marmara after a delightful island picnic, in the Naval
Attaché's launch, the sky suddenly began to darken. It was
pretty obvious that a line squall, unusual in this area, was
coming between us and the landing stage at Bebek. Both the
families on board the boat, the Naval Attaché's and the
Assistant Naval Attaché's, were not unduly perturbed as there
was only about two miles to go to disembarkation and
mooring.

When it came, however, the storm was extremely violent,
the wind and sea rose almost instantly, lightning flashed and
the visibility closed in the heavy rain to about 20 yards. The
Naval launch was no deep-sea boat, so we throttled back and
lay hove-to into the wind and sea.

Suddenly, down the starboard side drifted an open Turkish
rowing boat, half full of water, with a number of distressed
picnickers huddling down for shelter behind the low
gunwales and shouting for help. We increased the engine
power and turned across the sea to get alongside and take the
Turks off. We tried to throw a line to the rowing boat but in a
flash it missed its destination and, as usual, wound abaft
tightly around the starboard propellor, jamming the shaft
tight. The situation had now changed dramatically and it was
only by violent use of the remaining engine that we managed
to get both boats alongside each other.

The Turks were transferred to the Naval launch, a fresh line
passed to the rowing boat and within twenty minutes the line
squall had passed.

The British Naval Attaché was Captain Nigel Dixon and

his Assistant, Commander Pritchard. The former became the Director of the Royal National Life-boat Institution and the latter the National Appeals Secretary. In the Navy we call this 'Sod's Law', but no doubt the hand of fate is a better way of putting it.

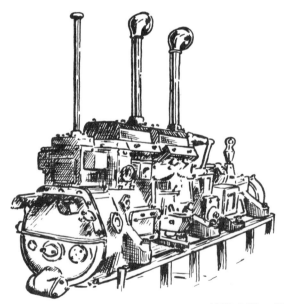

1930's Lifeboat Marine Engine

Ludovic Kennedy

WRITER AND BROADCASTER

It happened on one of those nasty Arctic convoys to North Russia, when it was dark for twenty hours out of twenty-four and so cold the sea froze as it landed on the deck and had to be chipped off with axes.

The one event we looked forward to in the wardroom each day was dinner. Luckily we had a very enterprising messman who fed us magnificently on the equivalent of about half-a-crown a day. He'd been messman in the ship in peacetime, and wherever we happened to be, still insisted on giving us a written menu, with the most flowery names for quite ordinary dishes.

One night, bumping up and down off Bear Island, we had a savoury, which was described on the menu as 'Rêve de Debussy'. The first lieutenant thought the messman had gone too far, called him in and told him so. The messman looked crestfallen.

However, he got his own back. By the time we had spent five days in Murmansk and started off on the return journey, we were down to the very basic rations. Yak appeared in a variety of guises, also Russian bread, the colour of tar and consistency of frayed rubber.

Then, one evening, the savoury that we had on the outward voyage appeared again. Eagerly we looked at the menu. Where 'Rêve de Debussy' had been written formerly, we now read, 'Tinned Sardines on Fried Bread'.

We all agreed, it didn't taste half so good.

Dame Naomi James DBE

AUTHOR AND YACHTSWOMAN

The following extract is from Dame Naomi's book At One with the Sea *(Hutchinson 1979).*

Express Crusader, the 53-ft sloop in which she was, single-handed, sailing round the World, was lying-a-hull in a gale with damaged rigging, halfway between New Zealand and Cape Horn:

On the 27th, that which I had always dreaded happened. Hours later I wrote in my log:

I capsized at 0.500 this morning. I was only half awake at the time, but suddenly aware that the wind had increased even beyond the prevailing force ten. It was just daylight and I was trying to make up my mind whether to get up and try steering when I heard the deafening roar of an approaching wave. I felt the shock, a mountain of water crashed against *Crusader*'s hull, and over she went. An avalanche of bits and pieces descended on me as she went under, and I put up my arms to protect my face. After a long and agonizing pause she lurched up again. I don't recall the act of climbing out of my bunk or even my sleeping bag but I found myself well and truly free of them both.

As far as I remember, my first move was to look through the skylight at the rigging. It scarcely registered that the mast was still standing. I could hear water running into the bilges, so I quickly started to pump. For a terrible moment, I felt that she was sinking, but as I pumped I could see the level going down. I pumped in a frenzy for a few minutes and then jumped on deck to see if the mast and rigging were really all right.

18

I noticed one spinnaker pole had gone and the other was broken. The sails which had been lashed along the guard rails were dragging in the water. I hauled them aboard somehow and re-tied them to the rails. The radio aerial was flying loose, and the deck fitting from which it had been torn was now letting in water. As a temporary measure I plugged it with an old T-shirt and returned below to continue pumping the bilges. There was a strong smell of paraffin and milk. All the stores on the top deck had been hurled out and the lee-cloth hung in shreds. My main concern was that she might go over again, so I left things below as they were, dug out some thick socks, gloves, hat and oilskins (all wet) and went to the helm to steer.

I secured my safety harness to the compass binnacle and faced the waves so that I could see them coming. The vision scared me stiff. The waves were gigantic, a combination of twenty-foot swells with twenty to thirty-foot waves on top. One crashed near by, and it didn't need any imagination to realize what would happen if one of these monsters fell on me.

Suddenly *Crusader* started to surf, and I gripped the wheel desperately to keep the stern directly on to the wave and hold her straight. The next wave picked her up like a toy and wrenched all control from me. There was nothing but mountains of water everwhere, like waterfalls. The speed was impossible to gauge as there was nothing to judge it by, and the water all round me was at deck level, seething and hissing as if on the boil. Finally, the wave passed and she slowed down. I started to cry from a feeling of helplessness at being out of control and caught at the mercy of one of those awful waves. But I still had to leave the wheel to pump the bilges. When I got back to the wheel a wave broke over the stern, and I threw my arms round the binnacle as the water cascaded over me and filled the cockpit. Fortunately the volume of water wasn't too alarming. What was the lesser evil, I wondered: capsizing or being crushed by a wave? What would Rob do? Keep on top of the situation and trust to luck. I had to accept the dismal thought that there was only me here with my quota of luck; I steered numbly onwards and hoped that my luck would last.

On the fourth occasion that I went below to pump I saw the barometer was 1003 and rising slowly. I was confronted by a terrible mess, but the biggest things had held in place; there was no actual damage except for odd dents and scars on the roof of the saloon. My neck was very sore – somehow I must have pulled a muscle at the moment of capsize because I was aware of aches as soon as I reached the deck.

I steered on devoid of thought and incapable of feeling. At 10.30 a.m. I detected a lull, followed half an hour later by another. At last I began to feel better, and when on a trip below I saw a bottle of port rolling in a corner and took a swig. I also grabbed some water biscuits and ate them at the wheel.

At 11.30 the wind was down to force eight, but I kept steering until 2 p.m., by which time the wind had reduced to intermittent heavy squalls. It now seemed safe, so I left her lying-a-hull. The radio was drenched but it worked, and after an hour of concentrated cleaning up the interior was almost back to normal. However, there seemed to be a curious itinerary of missing items, including my fountain pen, the can opener, hairbrush and kettle. Most of my crockery was broken. A bad moment was finding my Salalite transistor quite dead; that meant no more time signals to check the error of my chronometer. Still the clock was quartz and kept very good time, and there was no reason to think it might suddenly become erratic.

My bed was sopping wet, but fortunately I had a spare sleeping bag stowed away in a plastic bag. I hauled it out in triumph – bone dry! The cabin heater soon dried out my pillow. I had no dry footwear and on the floor was a slippery mixture of milk, paraffin and bilge water.

After clearing up I made myself a cup of tea and heated some tomato soup. I then slept for an hour but only fitfully as I could hear water dripping into the bilges. I finally stirred

myself and found that the water was coming from the hole in
the deck where the insulator had been. The best I could do was
to fill it with more rags until the weather improved. At 5 p.m.
the wind strength was force eight again, but the seas were
settling down and within two hours the barometer had begun
to climb. The weather might have improved but I still felt
very shaky.

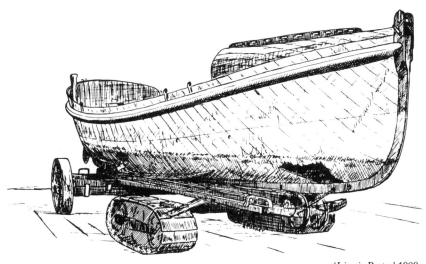

'Lizzie Porter' 1909

The Rt Hon Lord Mancroft
KBE TD MA

FORMER DEPUTY CHAIRMAN,
CUNARD LINE LIMITED

I am probably one of your few contributors, who, as a child, helped the horses pull the Cromer life-boat up the beach and was taught how to gut and clean a crab by its Cox'n, Harry Blogg, GC.

Some years ago, when I was Deputy Chairman and Managing Director of the Cunard Line, I was one of those responsible for the sale of the *Queen Mary* to the City of Long Beach, California.

The sale was negotiated over brunch in the St Regis Hotel, New York and the original contract was drafted and signed on the back of the menu. That menu is now framed on the wall of one of the ship's restaurants where she lies alongside in Long Beach Harbour, acting as an entertainment centre and museum of the sea.

We contracted to sell everything in the ship 'down to the last teaspoon' with the exception of Queen Mary's own personal Standard which she had very kindly presented to the ship when she launched her and which had to be returned to the Palace.

When I flew over to visit the *Queen Mary* during her reconditioning, I was greeted by an indignant Mayor who shocked me by saying 'You have broken your contract'. Contritely I enquired what had gone wrong.

'Well', he said, 'when the ship arrived here after her voyage round The Horn, we found that there wasn't a single teaspoon on board.'

It wasn't really our fault. Souvenir hunters had pinched the lot. But we had to send out four huge crates of teaspoons by air. It cost us a fortune and when we came to sell the *Queen Elizabeth*, my colleagues said would I kindly keep out of it and leave the negotiations to the lawyers.

Cliff Michelmore CBE

TELEVISION BROADCASTER AND PRODUCER

The charter had been arranged by telephone and when we got to Baltimore in the south of Ireland we saw her for the first time. A tub of a boat but good enough to take us out to the Fastnet Rock where we were to film the yachts in the Fastnet Race rounding the point and heading back.

We had to haggle and re-negotiate the terms of our charter because there was another film crew also looking for a boat and we were being gazumped. Eventually we were ready to cast off. The engine started, a hatch was drawn aside. One of the crew lowered a broom down into the engine well, one stood forward and another aft ready to cast off sharply. It was a case of hooking the broomhead around the throttle, lifting it, and simultaneously casting off. With a swerve or two and a cough from the engine we left the dockside.

Now the Fastnet is not all that far off the coast, so we were not all that worried when it transpired that we did not have a compass and our only radio contact was the set that *we* had brought with us to communicate with a couple of the boats in the race. After a while we made straight for one of the guard and escort boats, the *Chrysanthemum* if memory serves me right. The broom was once more lowered into the engine well and the throttle slowed us down to a drift.

Our skipper hailed the officer on watch. 'Could you give me a bearing to the Fastnet?'

'Yes', came the reply.

'No hang on', said our skipper, 'you see we haven't got a compass that works, could you just point the way and we'll take it from there.'

The escort vessel came on to a heading. 'It's in that direction.'

'Thank you very much.' We opened up the engine and we ran a course parallel to the ship's side and we were off. At last we found the Rock, a little late, as we had missed the first boat around, but we caught the main fleet. It was time for me to beat back to Baltimore and London with the first film rolls for developing. A motor launch found us, and I was off, leaving the rest of the crew to their fate.

It was a week before I met the film director again. 'Can you believe it? We got lost on the way back, found the entrance to the harbour and then we sat outside all night in case we ran on to those rocks. Early next morning we came in. And hit the rocks. I've only just got back.'

David Dimbleby

FREELANCE BROADCASTER AND
NEWSPAPER PROPRIETOR

Most sailors' lives at sea are packed with incident. Mine is rather different. I try if possible to avoid incident, so far successfully. I sail neither for the thrill of rounding the final mark in the lead, nor the satisfaction of making a perfect landfall, nor to test myself against the elements. I sail for peaceful relaxation and for the calming effect of being out of reach of telephones. My excitement, because it is always exciting, comes from the beauty of sailing, the sights and sounds.

My other sea journeys are in car ferries or liners. I once made a film about a party of ballroom dancing fanatics who had leased a small cruise liner to sail and dance from Southampton to Tangier and back. Cruise liner is a misnomer. She was a flat-bottomed car ferry which rolled so abominably that on another voyage water had gone down her funnel and put out of action all her electrical systems.

For several days we had filmed the clouds of net and tulle as they swirled on the ballroom floor, but one sequence had been left until the end. I was to be taught the tango. On the day chosen for this hazardous enterprise it was blowing a full gale in the Bay of Biscay. Meals and dancing had come to an end, but filming must always go on.

Now the tango is a tricky dance, consisting of many twists and turns, and curious jerky movements backwards and forwards – not the thing for a delicate stomach, and not at all the thing for a full-gale in the forward lounge. My partner arrived clutching a sick-bag just in case, We executed a number of turns for the camera, clutching the bag between us so that it could not be seen by the lens. On our final dizzying run across the sloping deck the pace was too much. My partner executed a perfect whirl and spin, and vomited into the bag. Sadly this incident went unrecorded in the final film.

Sir Peter Parker MVO

FORMER CHAIRMAN,
BRITISH RAILWAYS BOARD

In my job I have to tour a great deal and this means leaping in and out of trains and cars – and this is what I was doing on a trip in Ireland. On that particular unforgettable trip I split my trousers and there was simply no way of holding everybody up and we had a Sealink ship to catch to Holyhead. I walked up the gangplank with an uncharacteristically stiff gait to make sure that my suit jacket covered the Irish Channel of a gap that had appeared up the seat of my trousers.

On the ship I quietly asked the purser for what I thought was a brilliant solution: using a stapler, so that the rest of my tour at Holyhead could go on as planned. At rest those staples did a fine job, but when, with renewed confidence, I strode off on the Holyhead tour and found myself jumping in and out of cars, the staples gave way and when I finally got into the train and on to my seat I found myself sitting on what seemed to be a crown of thorns.

If I had made the crossing in a sailing ship I would naturally have asked for some help from a needle and thread – it is the worst sign of bureaucracy that I should have asked for a stapler.

Anthony Bowring

TRANSGLOBE EXPEDITION

On Easter Day 1982, Sir Ranulph Fiennes and Charles Burton reached the North Pole. As the leading members of the Transglobe Expedition, they had made history by being the first team to travel on the ice to both South and North Poles. Their route over the past three years had been by land, sea and ice around the world, following a longitudinal track. This took them across the Sahara and the tropical jungles of West Africa, by sea to the Antarctic and, over a period of 14 months, across the Antarctic.

In early 1981, Ran and Charlie steamed up the Pacific on board the expedition ship m.v. *Benjamin Bowring* and entered the Bering Sea. By Dunlop inflatable they travelled 800 miles up the Yukon River and by 18-ft open whaler they negotiated the infamous North-West Passage. The final stage was to cross the Arctic. With temperatures down to −53°C, they came out from their base camp in northern Ellesmere Island. Despite a fire at base camp which destroyed all their spare equipment and a near fatal accident when Ranulph's skidoo and sledge fell through the ice to a watery grave, the team reached the North Pole and continued their journey towards Spitsbergen. At 86°N the warm temperatures were causing an early break up of the ice and they resolved to remain on a solid ice floe which was slowly drifting South.

The *Benjamin Bowring* was ready and waiting at Spitsbergen to steam up into the ice and rendezvous with Ran and Charlie. The success of the 'pick-up' was always considered doubtful but an attempt was made.

The weeks passed and the ice team drifted slowly South. Sometimes they managed to cover five miles in a day but occasionally in a strong Southerly wind they actually drifted back to the North. When atmospheric conditions allowed, we received radio reports on their position and temperatures, the latter remained warm enough to prevent solid ice forming from the 'porridge ice' and indeed melted water pools began to form on the floe. As they were still unable to travel across the ice they simply had to wait patiently and rely on the slow drift of the ice.

Occasionally our twin 'Otter' aircraft would fly out to drop supplies to Ran and Charlie. From Longyearbyen it was a three-hour flight. Once clear of the Spitsbergen coast a view of open water was visible below. At 80 °N a belt of loosely-broken ice appeared. Depending on the wind direction, below this, ice could be either closely-packed or, in a Northerly wind, it could be opened up and reasonably accessible to the ship. Immediately after this ice edge more solid floes would appear with narrow leads of water separating them. Further North the floes became larger and the water less. One floe was about 80 miles across. At this stage the ship would be stopped unless leads could be found to provide access to the North East. By 82°N there was almost no evidence of water and the ice seemed very solid indeed. Mile after mile of ice passed below the aircraft. Occasional pools of water and cracks in the ice would appear but in effect the seemingly white landscape was a jumble of broken floes with boulders of the ice thrust up into walls by the immense pressure caused by the Gyral Current which forces the frozen crust of the Arctic Ocean out into the Greenland Sea.

When about 50 miles from the ice team's camp, the plaintive tone of the homing beacon could be picked up and before long an experienced eye could pick the hard black dots of the tents out from the featureless scene below. It is hard to imagine what it must have been like to live so many miles from land and to watch the slow movement of the ice as you drifted imperceptibly counting the minutes and degrees of latitude from 86°N to the open sea. To travel West of the Greenwich Meridian could mean getting caught in the belt of ice which follows the East coast of Greenland for many further miles to the South. A constant problem was the frequent visits of Polar bears who were always inquisitive and, despite their placid expressionless faces, they were a very serious danger to Ran and Charlie. For 99 days the two of them lived on their floe. They each had their own tent and two canoes were ready and loaded with emergency supplies in case the mush around them turned into open leads of water or the floe broke up and left them homeless.

Once overhead the aircraft would do a low pass and through the open cargo door fresh supplies and equipment could be dropped. The Omega Navigation System on the aircraft provided confirmation of the position which they had reached which was a great asset as Ran was seldom able to take a sight of the sun with the sky frequently being overcast or, worse still, with the seasonal thick fog which often enveloped them.

While this long drift was going on, the *Benjamin Bowring* was waiting ever patiently in Longyearbyen. A scientific programme for Southampton University was carried out in Isfjørd and then the ship set out to navigate the ice edge and discover just how penetrable the ice really was. Our first attempt was surprisingly successful. We headed North West from the Spitsbergen coast and steamed through a wide opening in the ice edge. We continued to follow wide open leads and with only a few strikes at the ice managed to reach some 60 miles beyond the ice edge before ending up in a cul-de-sac with no evidence of an exit apart from retracing our course. Back at the ice edge we followed it to the South West and found it to be impenetrable.

Sadly, at this time, the team were still far too far to the North for us to retrieve them and so we returned to Spitsbergen. We had a second trial which proved to be less successful. We managed to push through the edge but soon got stuck amongst heavy floes. To make a successful rendezvous with the team we realised that for the ship to get beset in the ice would be unwise. Inevitably we would have to push our way into the ice and aim for Ran and Charlie but were we to get stuck we might find leads opening further afield with better access to the North and thus the ship would be unable to make use of such an opportunity until it was freed from its entangled situation. To remain mobile at the ice edge would allow us to move quickly when a lead did open up and use it to our advantage. The trouble is that the lie of the ice changes so quickly and frequently it is difficult to have theories and you end up moving when you can and unexpectedly stopping when you can't!

However, our third attempt was lucky. With only a small improvement in the ice conditions we decided to set out again and if necessary sit off the ice-ridge until it opened up enough for us to pass. We were constantly blinkered by fog which formed from the relatively warm summer air and the very cold water. We made progress when we could and stopped when we could not see the ice around us. In the clearer weather, open leads were often identifiable in the distance by the dark reflection that they cast on the low clouds above. Making our way towards those leads could often take hours. Progress between two floes was inevitably hampered by wedges of ice which would neither break nor be swept aside by the thrust of our bows and the draw of water from our propeller. Patience was required to overcome the frustration caused by these small floes and a degree of skill was necessary to use the ungainly hull to advantage. However, slowly and surely, we moved on into the ever-changing landscape of ice. When visibility allowed, the twin 'Otter' flew out to guide us from above. Often a promising route could be seen from the air while below the ship would crawl imperceptibly gnawing away at the floes which barred our progress. The shuddering and grinding of the hull in the ice was a constant accompaniment as we moved and the lurching and jolting was often enough to throw us off balance.

Mile after mile we crawled on, closing the gap between the team and their ship. As we got closer the mood on board the

Benjamin Bowring was getting all the more cheerful. Like the final lap of a race, we were determined to push on with mounting excitement and on a day when the clouds were high and visibility was good, Karl reported that he was flying over Ran and Charlie and could see the ship in the distance. When we were only 15 miles from our goal the ice-bound duo decided to move and with their heavily-laden canoes, they set off hauling them over the lumps and bumps of ice and paddling across the water and slush. The sun broke out from behind the clouds and snow was falling gently. Ran reported that he could see the ship when he stood on a towering pinnacle of ice, his voice crackling over the portable radio. Everyone on board was up and about and the mast, crows nest and the rigging were full of bodies straining their eyes through binoculars to catch a glimpse of the tiny figures leaning into their harnesses and heaving at the canoes. It was certainly the most exciting moment of the journey as success at this stage was looking possible and yet we all had doubts that such a recovery could be performed without helicopters and all our advisers had shown considerable concern and not much optimism.

The ship crawled on through boulders of ice while Ran and Charlie heaved their loads towards us. The wind shifted to the North and a fresh breeze had picked up. The ice was just letting us through. We were now five miles apart and everyone on board the ship had a searching look to see the tiny specks disappear and re-emerge from behind the massive blocks of ice which dotted the horizon.

The ship finally came to a halt just seven miles from the floe which had been home to Ran and Charlie for 99 days. Before long the two of them were clearly visible to the naked eye and the effort to haul the canoes became apparent. Once stopped, it required them to jerk with all their might at the harnesses to get the canoes under way and to break the grip of the ice on the aluminium hulls. With less than half-a-mile to go, Ran stopped and Charlie came up beside him. Ran busied himself with the cover of his boat and before long had a Union Jack unfurled and flying from a short mast on his canoe. This done, they resumed their task and covered the last leg of their lonely journey across the ice.

From loudspeakers on board the ship, we played *The Eton Boating Song* (Ran is an old Etonian) and followed it with *Land of Hope and Glory*. There was much shouting and cheering from the ship as the two tired explorers stood at the side of the ship and the bellow of Charlie's laughter exploded amongst the cheers. Ten years ago it was an idea, and on this day, 4th August 1982, at 00.14 hours in the middle of a vast expanse of Arctic ice at 80 31' North and 0 59' West, the work was done.

For the next ten days the *Benjamin Bowring* was locked in the ice. We made a few efforts to push our way out but the ice had closed up behind us and we had to wait for it to open again. Slowly, we continued the drift South, which Ran and Charlie understood so well and with advice from the twin 'Otter' we finally emerged into open water and in less than a day at sea were back in Spitsbergen.

On August 29th the *Benjamin Bowring* returned to this country and sailed proudly up the Thames with the Expedition's Patron H.R.H. Prince Charles, on board, only four days short of 2nd September, which in 1979 was the departure day before this great adventure began.

Deborah Kerr

ACTRESS

I wish it were possible for me to contribute something amazing – amusing or just worth telling, for the wonderful cause you are raising money for!

Amazing as it may seem, in all the *years* I crossed the Atlantic, in those glorious days when one always took the *Queen Mary* or the *Queen Elizabeth,* or the *Nieuw Amsterdam* or the *Michelangelo* to New York and back, and also having had ten marvellous years owning a 32-foot Fairy Marine Swordsman power boat, which we keep in Marbella, Spain, *nothing* unusual or amazing has ever happened! Unless, of course, if *I* caught the biggest fish of the day, which would drive our sailor (who is a fisherman!) absolutely berserk!

I adore being on the sea and am a maniac about fishing, and I have spent many happy hours tirelessly trying to catch the 'big one' of the day! You can imagine my pride if I *do*! Particularly with a professional fisherman on board!

If any of this is in any way useful, please use it with my name.

Commander Peter D Sturdee
OBE RN (Ret'd)

HON. CURATOR
NATIONAL LIFE-BOAT MUSEUM

A few days after the convoy escort vessel in which I was the Sub Lieutenant had sunk a U-boat and rescued her crew on St Patrick's Day 1941, the German crew came to my cabin to claim their personal belongings. The items had been dried out and inspected, letters read, and anything of intelligence value removed for sending to the Admiralty. All these effects had been laid out on my bunk and were handed back to their owners with the agreement of the German Petty Officer, who was also acting as my interpreter. Through him I chatted to some of the Germans about their family photographs, particularly those of girl-friends and wives.

When all the crew had been to my cabin my bunk was clear, except for a rosary and a medallion of The Virgin Mary on a neck chain, which had been left unclaimed. Then a fellow officer called out from the top of the ladder leading to my cabin, that two Germans were very anxious to collect their belongings. I called them down. Two young and embarrassed seamen stepped nervously into the cabin and whispered to the Petty Officer. Suddenly something took charge of me, prompted no doubt by the ship's recent victory in trumping the top U-boat ace.

In my best quarterdeck voice I demanded to know what the two seamen wanted; as if I didn't know. My interpreter replied: 'Sur they have come for the rosary and medallion'. I replied that I was not there for their convenience and why had they not taken them before? 'But Sur, these men are Catholics. If they had taken those things in front of the uzzers they would have been molested . . . possibly killed!'

It was a rather shaken, humble and thoughtful Sub Lieutenant who turned to pick up the rosary and medallion. I shall never forget the look those two German seamen gave me as they gratefully received back the two symbols of their faith.

For that brief moment the four of us were just seamen in the same ship.

Michael Nicholson

INDEPENDENT TELEVISION NEWS

It was my first D-Day landing and, naturally, I was a little apprehensive. It isn't, after all, the kind of thing anyone does regularly and it isn't something you could ever get used to.

San Carlos Water, off the Falklands Sound, May 21st 1982, and the British Forces of the Task Force were going ashore from their assault ships to push the Argies off the islands they had no right to be on.

Four-thirty in the morning, pitch black outside, the rumble of the diesel engines of the landing craft coming up alongside us, and four hundred men of 40 Marine Commando huddled below on the tank deck of the RFA *Stromness*. Above us the booming of guns, and we not knowing whether it was our shells going out or theirs coming in.

They were all young lads, their faces blacked, their helmets covered in half an English hedgerow and, as they were infantrymen and about to wade into the unknown, they carried an enormous weight of ammo in bandoliers and pouches.

There was a delay. There'd been an accident with one of the

landing craft carrying the Paras and the whole shuttle had been held up. The sound of the guns shook the ship, the last cigarette had been smoked, men stopped chatting to each other, they were feeling suddenly very alone and very vulnerable. The tension was dreadful. Suddenly the Company Sergeant Major, short back and sides and lantern jawed, just as they are in the movies, shouted out, 'Nowacks'.

'Yes Sir?'

'Stand up Nowacks.'

Nowacks stood up. He was a small lad, but very stocky and I reckon if he had been just a few inches wider he'd have been square! His eyes sparkled from the black camouflaged face.

The CSM walked two paces forward. 'What's that you're wearing Nowacks?'

'It's a bra, Sir.'

'A bra Nowacks?'

'A bra Sir.'

'And why, may I ask' asked the CSM in the most beautifully precise and Ealing Studios fashion, 'are you wearing a bra?'

With great timing and an enormous grin, Private Nowacks paused and replied 'It's every Marine's right to wear a bra Sir!'

And with a great roar of approval from the men, the CSM grinned back and said 'Too bloody right it is lad, and when this is over, I'll give you a medal to pin on them'.

It was just what we needed, and within minutes the Marines were climbing down the rope netting with their packs and guns into the landing craft that were to take them to war.

I reckon Private Nowacks would have got his medal too. But he was killed in action on Two Sisters the night before that white flag flew over Port Stanley. . . .

Sir Christopher Cockerell
CBE FRS

INVENTOR OF THE HOVERCRAFT

I enclose a copy of a letter which I wrote to my father, Sir Sydney Cockerell LittD, about the first crossing of the SRN 6 hovercraft from Calais to Dover on the 50th anniversary of Blériot's flight. Strangely enough, Commander Peter Lamb, who drove the SRN 6, was a nephew of the first journalist who reached Blériot when he landed on the cliffs of Dover.

August 15th, 1959

Dearest Father,

Many thanks for your letter, and of course for the telegram addressed to Hovercraft, Dover! I have had a quite appalling lot of letters to write, and a ghastly lot of people writing to ask me to give lectures, three from the U.S.A., one of which I have accepted. So I am off to Princeton University on about October 20th for about a week.

It goes well, although I think we are all a bit tired as a result of the pace over the last year, and now we must slow down a bit and take stock of the situation.

The Channel crossing was quite fun, but really we were lucky to get away with it. We flew to a R.A.F. aerodrome near Dover on Thursday afternoon, stayed in a Folkestone hotel – but the Press found us – got up very early – not much breakfast as hotels can't operate out of hours these days; crossed to Calais in a R.A.F. Air-Sea Rescue launch, and arrived at the same time as the Hovercraft, which was on the Admiralty lighter. The French were most helpful, but there was too much wind, so we went out into the middle of the Channel in an

Admiralty tug, and wallowed about observing the sea conditions, and returned about 4 p.m. By this time, there were pretty big crowds, and so we decided that we would have to give some sort of demonstration, so we flew about the harbour, and then went out of the harbour and headed for the sands and beach, which were covered with a mass of people. So we came in rather slowly, and the people divided as we went up and over the sands and round about, the people melting before us and coming together behind us.

We turned and went a little way out to sea and then came in again and repeated the operation.

This demonstration relieved the pressure on us, so we went off into Calais for some food. Lamb and I slept in the sick bay on the tug – slept, the portholes looked out onto the quay, and merry sailors and others stood around and effectively prevented sleep. We were up at 4 a.m. and went out of the harbour in the R.A.F. Launch (with only a third of the crew! the rest having been mislaid in Calais), to observe the sea and wind. Then back again and on to the Hovercraft, and off we went. It was only just light, and there was mist about.

There was little wind at the start, only a swell, and we skimmed along very nicely, I lying on the foredeck to help to counterbalance the weight of extra petrol, which was in tanks aft. Nothing to be seen except sea and sea and sea, and I was getting wetter and wetter, and drinking in more and more salt spray – but it was quite exhilarating skimming up the swell and rushing down the other side.

Quite suddenly I looked up, and there, faintly, were the cliffs of Dover, I suppose about ten miles off. There was wind now, and a bit of a chop on the swell, and a little later there was a motor boat crossing our path. We stopped and then went on again.

The R.A.F. launch had come out with us and was close

at hand on our port quarter. Little Press aircraft began to appear, flying at nought feet, and just about clipping us, and I wondered if we would have to do some air-sea rescue work.

Still the cliffs of Dover, but there was quite a chop, and wind, and we weren't going very fast, and I was getting cold and feeling a bit muzzy due to all the salt, no breakfast, and not much sleep. We were about a mile off Dover, we stopped to transfer the spare petrol we carried in cans to the tanks; and then off we went at a good clip, and into the harbour and across it, and there was the beach, the very steep beach of shingle.

Up the beach we went, and the craft came to rest at such an angle that I fell off the back along with a couple of petrol cans. Then – the crowds and the Press, and a broadcast, and autographs – but much more important, something to eat and a bath and dry clothes. It's the physical things that one feels at the time.

Looking back, I think it was worth doing, it is chalked up as a first anywhere, which I suppose is worth something, and according to my friend John has caused the conservative old salts to take a look at the thing.

We have had enquiries for river hovercraft, and land hovercraft, and amphibious hovercraft, and hovercraft ferries and Arctic hovercraft and military hovercraft and ocean hovercraft – this would want a whole industry to do it justice – in fact there are only about a dozen trained hovercraft engineers in the country, so we are still in danger of letting a glorious export opportunity go by default. The National Research Development Corporation are working at it, but the situation requires no less than a modern Disraeli.

I hope to come to see you again soon.

Hammond Innes *CBE*

AUTHOR AND TRAVELLER

We were headed for Omonville-la-Rogue just west of Cherbourg and had arrived off the French coast about midnight. Rather than enter this very small port at night, I decided to stand on and off until daylight. Accordingly, we shortened sail and headed seaward. We went into single watches and from my bunk in the quarter-berth I could see the helmsman's face under a yellow sou'wester lit by the binnacle light. It was a dark night.

I relieved him at 02.00. As I came up through the hatch, he had just completed putting the yacht about again. Over his shoulder I could see a strange, green translucence in the sea. It looked for all the world like some monster of the deep surfacing and trailing its phosphorescence with it.

'What the hell's that?' I asked, pointing aft. He turned, and in that moment the green translucence became brighter, gradually hardening into a pinpoint of emerald green. I knew what it was then.

'My God! A ship!'

And it was close, very close. Not more than two cables off. And only then did we get the first faint rumble of its engines. At first sighting it might have been a ghost ship. But now other lights appeared, port-hole lights as well as that starb'd navigation light, all iridescent and pale in the fog. I hadn't realised we were in fog.

And as it went sliding past our stern I thought to myself – what if it really had been a ghost ship? What if there had been nobody up there on the high bridge, nobody at the helm? What a marvellous opening for a book – a freighter driving up-Channel and nobody in command, nobody on board, a sort of beat-up old tramp of a *Marie Celeste*.

I went back down to the chart table to enter the near miss in the log book and at the same time my personal reaction to the sudden appearance of what I was fairly certain must be one of the Channel Island ferries.

That was the origin of the opening scene of *The Wreck of the Mary Deare*.

'North Foreland' 1951

Stanley Nelson *(no relation)*

DESIGNER

The first and only time I received severe punishment, RN style, was the result of attaining my 19th birthday, compounded by the (then) tradition surrounding the 'tot' issue of awarding 'sippers' to messmates for minor favours like lending them your last few quid to go ashore, to the ultimate 'gulpers' on more significant occasions.

Rum, even as grog and mostly water, was a pretty potent beverage to one of such tender years, and the haven of the oilskin locker midships seemed a good idea for the rest of the forenoon as there was no work to be done until my first watch at first dog.

Behind the densely-packed oilskins was a 3' × 6' ledge which exactly accommodated a messdeck cushion, the perfect resting place for the slightly inebriated.

It must have been around 16.30 when the fatherly hand of the bosun brought a faintly apprehensive awakening which quickly developed into a blood-draining-down-to-the-deck-slippers sensation as the enormity of the crime of being missing on watch was realised. Added to this was the awful silence – gone was the familiar throb of engines. . . .

'We all thought you had gone overboard, lad', was wistfully expressed, 'you'd better go on "Captain's".'

Next Sunday morning 'Off caps' led to a sentence of fourteen days 'captain of the heads' from the skipper who turned out to be a student of colour psychology. 'Not only will you clean them, you will also paint the walls', he said. 'Deckhead bright blue, bulkheads orange.'

Despite the lack of privacy (the lower deck's heads on this destroyer was simply a row of half-a-dozen pedestals) certain crew members habitually sat, literally cheek to cheek for much longer than necessary to perform the usual function, spending time reading, doing football pools or simply in conversation.

This bilious colour combination was designed to dissuade the practice by its sheer sickening effect. It didn't work. . . .

Bryan Forbes

ACTOR, FILM DIRECTOR, PRODUCER
AND WRITER

Many years ago I was acting in a film called *The Key,* directed by the late Sir Carol Reed. Together with William Holden and Trevor Howard we set out every morning from Weymouth in an ocean-going tug to recreate some war-time mayhem in the Portland Race – a stretch of water not noted for its soothing effect on landlubbers like me. Sir Carol was seasick every day and although the rest of us gradually became vaguely professional seagoing folk (we were at it for some eight or nine weeks) I can't pretend that we looked upon the experience as a way of life!

At one point the script called for a German U-Boat to surface quite close to the tug, and for the purpose of recreating the scene the Royal Navy 'lent' us an operational submarine.

Now Sir Carol was a great film director, totally unaware , during the making of a film, of any external factors unconnected with the job in hand. So on this particular day he lined up a shot on Bill Holden and myself and then told his assistant director to convey his wishes through a loud-hailer to the submarine commander.

'Tell him it's an absolutely marvellous shot, and that I want him to submerge and then surface on that exact spot.'

The assistant looked a little dubious, as did we all, but faithfully signalled Sir Carol's instructions.

Back across the water came a very Royal Navy rejoinder: 'Are you some sort of lunatic?'

'What's he say?' Sir Carol asked.

'I don't think he's too happy about the idea, Carol.'

'But it'll make a wonderful shot,' Carol said, taking another handful of seasick pills. 'Explain it to him again.'

This was duly done. The submarine commander was having none of it. 'I couldn't surface within half a mile', he shouted back. 'And furthermore, I don't intend to.' And with that he closed the conning tower and disappeared beneath the waves.

We never did get the shot and I don't think Carol ever quite understood the difficulty. 'Would have won the Academy Award that shot', he muttered. He was right of course; had he been able to start on an empty sea, catch the phoney U-Boat surfacing and then pan the camera to include Bill and myself on the bridge of a tug which was standing on end, there is no doubt that cinema history would have been made. But, sadly, it wasn't.

Sir Peter Scott CBE DSC

ARTIST AND CHAIRMAN OF THE WORLD
WILDLIFE FUND (INTERNATIONAL)

This extract from Sir Peter's book The Eye of the Wind *(Hodder &*
Stoughton) giving an account of a wartime fire at sea whilst he was
serving in HMS Broke, *a destroyer leader, is used with the author's*
permission. It has been slightly abridged.

On Sunday, 6th April, 1941, I came on watch at four p.m. for
the first dog watch and found a wild grey day of heavy seas,
driving squalls, and a moderate south-easterly gale.

We were on our way to meet a homeward-bound Gibraltar
convoy, having parted company with the outward-bound
convoy in the early morning, and we were plunging into a
head sea at seven knots which was as much as we could do
with comfort.

We were in company with *Douglas* (an old Destroyer
Leader like ourselves, and Senior Officer on this occasion) and
Salisbury (an ex-American destroyer) and our position was on
the port wing of a sweeping formation.

When I came to the bridge three other ships were in sight,
which was unusual because chance meetings were not
common in 21° West – 600 miles out in the Atlantic – more
especially on days of poor visibility like this one.

These three ships were already some way astern and
steering west, and I learned that we had 'spoken' to them half
an hour before when they had first come into sight. They
were HMS *Comorin* ex-P&O liner of 15,000 tons, now an
armed merchant cruiser, the *Glenartney*, a smaller merchant
ship, and *Lincoln,* another ex-American destroyer, who was
their escort.

They soon disappeared into the smoky haze and my watch
passed uneventfully.

About twenty minutes after I had been relieved I was informed in the wardroom that the starboard fore-topmast-backstay had parted, and I went at once to the bridge to organise the repair. While I was there a signal was received from *Lincoln* at six-twenty p.m.:

'HMS *Comorin* seriously on fire in position 54° 39′N, 21° 13′W join us if possible. 1600/6.

We passed this to *Douglas* for permission to go and were detached at six-forty.

Having told *Lincoln* by radio that we were coming, we made a further signal: 'Expect to sight you at 2015. Is a U-boat involved?' to which came: 'Reply No'.

During this time we were able to increase to eighteen knots and with the following sea the ship's motion was so much easier that the backstay was quickly repaired and secured. We then began making preparations for what might turn out to be our sixth load of survivors since war began.

Scrambling nets, lifebuoys, oil drums (to pour oil on to the troubled waters), heaving lines and heavier bow and stern lines for boats, line-throwing gun, grass line and manilla – all these were got ready and the mess decks were prepared for casualties.

At eight minutes past eight in the evening *Glenartney* was sighted fine on the port bow at extreme visibility range – about eight miles – and four minutes later *Comorin* was seen right ahead, which was exactly three minutes earlier than expected. There was a lot of white smoke coming from her single funnel.

We asked *Lincoln,* who was laying just to windward of the burning ship, what the situation was and she told us that *Comorin* was being abandoned, that no boats were left, that *Glenartney* was picking up some rafts and that she, *Lincoln,* was hauling over rafts on a grass line.

When we drew near the scene was awe-inspiring. The great liner lay beam on to the seas drifting very rapidly. A red glow showed in the smoke which belched from her funnel and below that amidships the fire had a strong hold. Clouds of smoke streamed away from her lee side. The crew were assembled aft and we were in communication by lamp and later by semaphore. From the weather quarter the *Lincoln's* Carley rafts were being loaded up – a dozen men at a time and hauled across to the destroyer lying about two cables away. It was a desperately slow affair and we went in close to see if we could not go alongside.

To go alongside *Comorin* seemed an impossibility. The waves were fifty to sixty feet from trough to crest and the liner's cruiser stern lifted high out of the water at one moment showing rudder and screws and crashed downwards in a cloud of spray the next. I thought a destroyer could not posibly survive such an impact. Finally their Captain made a signal that he thought the only chance was for *Broke* to go alongside and let the men jump. This was at nine-fifty p.m. By this time it was almost dark and the *Lincoln's* raft ferry had failed owing to the parting of their grass line. I do not know how many people they had rescued by this ferry, but it cannot have been very many as it was desperately slow. Not that it wasn't enormously worth doing, for at the time it seemed to be the only way at all.

Obviously a raft secured to the upper deck of a heavily rolling ship cannot be secured close alongside. If it were it would be hauled out of the water by its end whenever the ship rolled away and all those already embarked would be pitched out. The rafts therefore had to remain ten or fifteen yards from the *Comorin's* side and men had to go down the rope to them. It was here that several men were drowned.

As it gradually got dark the glow from the fire shone redly and eventually became the chief source of light. As soon as we knew we were going alongside I went down to the fo'c'sle, got all the fenders over to the port side, and had all the locker cushions brought up from the mess decks.

I suggested that hammocks should be brought up, but Angus Letty, our Navigating Officer, said that since it was still doubtful if we should get alongside he thought it would be a pity to get them all wet. I wish I had pressed the point but I didn't. Letty had been doing excellent work on the fo'c'sle all the time, but I think his judgment was at fault in this and so was mine in not seeing at once that he was wrong. What are a few wet hammocks by comparison with broken limbs?

So we closed the starboard (leeward) quarter of the *Comorin* and in a few minutes we had scraped alongside.

The absolutely bewildering thing was the relative speed that the ships passed each other in a vertical direction. The men waiting on the after promenade deck were forty feet above our fo'c'sle at one moment and at the next they were ten feet below. As they passed our fo'c'sle they had to jump as if jumping from an express lift.

The first chance was easy. About nine jumped and landed mostly on the fo'c'sle, some on B gun deck. They were all safe and uninjured. As they came doubling aft I asked them how they got on and they were cheerful enough.

One petty officer came with this lot – PO Fitzgerald – and I immediately detailed him to help with the organisation of survivors as they embarked.

There was little, if any, damage to the ship from this first encounter and we backed away to get into position for the next. As we closed in for the seond attempt the terrific speed of the rise and fall of the other ship in relation to our own fo'c'sle was again the main difficulty for the jumpers, added to which the ships were rolling in opposite directions, so that at one minute they touched, at the next they were ten yards apart. This very heavy rolling made it almost impossible for us to keep our feet on the fo'c'sle. We had to hold on tightly nearly all the time. I remember I had started the operation wearing a cap as I thought I should be easier to recognise that way, but I so nearly lost it in the gale that I left it in the wireless office for safe-keeping.

The second jump was much more difficult than the first. Only about six men came and three of them were injured.

From then I do not remember the chronology of events as one jump followed another with varying pauses for manoeuvring. Our policy was not to remain alongside for any length of time as this would have been very dangerous and might well have damaged us to the point of foundering in these monstrous seas. Instead we quickly withdrew after each brief contact in order to assess the damage and decide upon the seaworthiness of the ship before closing in again for another attempt.

The scene was lit chiefly by the fire, as it was now pitch dark. Occasionally the *Lincoln*'s searchlight swept across us as they searched the sea for the last Carley raft which had somehow broken adrift. At each successive jump a few more men were injured.

We decided to rig floodlights to light the fo'c'sle so that the men could judge the height of the jump. These were held by Leading Telegraphist Davies and Ordinary Seaman Timperon all the time. The pool of light which they formed gave the whole scene an extraordinary artificiality, as if this were some ghastly film scene and I can remember, as I stood impotently waiting for the next jump, feeling suddenly remote as if watching through the wrong end of a telescope.

As soon as the jumping men had begun to injure themselves I sent aft for the doctor who was in bed with a temperature. He came for'ard at once and started to work. At the third jump we drew ahead too far and the whaler at its davits was crushed but several men jumped into it and were saved that way. Another time the Captain changed his mind and decided to get clear by going ahead instead of astern. The ship was struck a heavy blow aft on the port for'ard depth charge thrower.

At this jump there had been a good many injured and as we went ahead into the sea again to circle *Comorin* for another approach the decks began to wash down with great seas. This was awkward for the disposal of the injured and I went up and asked the Captain if in future we could have a little longer to clear away and prepare for the next jump – to which he readily agreed.

My routine was to be down by 'A' gun for the jump. There was a strut to the gun-cover frame which was the best handhold. Here I saw that the padding was properly distributed, the light properly held, the stretcher parties in readiness and hands all ready to receive the survivors.

Then we would crash alongside for a few breathtaking seconds whilst the opportunity did or did not arise for a few to jump. Sometimes there would be two opportunities – first while we still went ahead, and then again as we came astern. The great thing was to get the injured away before the next people jumped on them. As soon as this had been done I went with the Shipwright to survey the damage and then up to report to the Captain. This was a rather exhausting round trip and before the end I got cramp in my right arm through over-exercise of the muscles.

The damage to the ship was at first superficial, consisting of dents in the fo'c'sle flare and bent guard-rails and splinter shields. But at length one bad blow struck us near the now-crushed whaler on the upper deck level. I ran aft and found a large rent in the ship's side out of which water was pouring. I did not think that the boiler room could have filled quickly enough for this to be sea water coming out again, and came to the conclusion that it was a fresh-water tank. This was later confirmed by the Shipwright. As I had thought, it was the port 'peace' tank. This was an incredible stroke of good fortune, as a hole of that size in the boiler room would have been very serious indeed in that sea.

Several of *Comorin*'s officers had now arrived and we began to get estimates of the numbers still to come. There seemed always to be an awful lot more. I detailed Lt Loftus to go down to the mess decks as chief receptionist and went back to my usual round – fo'c'sle for a jump, clear the injured, view the damage, report to the Captain and back to the fo'c'sle.

By now some of the injuries appeared to be pretty bad.

There were a good many broken legs and arms and one chap fell across the guard-rail from about twenty-five feet.

It filled me with gloom, and since at least one-third of the survivors landing on the fo'c'sle had to be carried off it, I became desperately worried by the high percentage of casualties. True, they had improved lately since we had ranged all available hammocks in rows, like sausages. They made very soft padding but a few ankles still slipped between them and got twisted.

On one of my round trips I met an RNVR Sub-Lieutenant survivor trying to get some photos of the burning ship (I never heard whether they came out). There were a good many officers on board by this time, mostly RNR. Of course they did not recognise me, hatless in duffle coat, grey flannel trousers and sea boots, and it took a few moments to persuade them to answer my searching questions.

Still the estimated number remaining did not seem to dwindle. Sometimes there were longish pauses while we manoeuvred into position. Twice we went alongside without getting any men at all. Once the ship came in head on and the stem was stove in, for about eight feet down from the bull ring, and we got no survivors that time either.

Somewhere around eleven-thirty p.m. the fire reached the rockets on the *Comorin* which went off splendidly, together with various other fireworks such as red Verey's Lights and so on. Later the small arms ammunition began to explode, at first in ones and twos and then in sharp rattles and finally in a continuous roar.

The sea was as bad as ever and at each withdrawal we had to go full astern into it. This meant that very heavy waves were sweeping the quarter-deck, often as high as the blast shield of X gun (about eight feet). When these waves broke over the ship she shuddered and set up a vibration which carried on often for twenty or thirty seconds. All this time the hull was clearly under great strain. As we got more used to going alongside some of my particular fears grew less, but the

51

apparent inevitability of casualties was a constant source of worry and there was also the continual speculation upon how much the ship would stand up to.

Once on the first approach there seemed to be a chance for a jump. Two men jumped, but it was too far and they missed. I was at the break of the fo'c'sle at the time, and looked down into the steaming, boiling abyss. With the two ships grinding together as they were there did not seem the slightest chance of rescuing them. More men were jumping now and theirs was the prior claim. The ship came ahead, men jumped on to the flag deck and the pom-pom deck amidships was demolished: then as we went astern, I ran again to the side to see if there was any sign of the two in the water, but there was none that I could see.

Having got the injured off the fo'c'sle I went aft to examine the damage to the pom-pom deck and see if the upper deck had been pierced. I heard a very faint cry of 'Help', and looking over the side saw that a man was holding on to the scrambling nets which I had ordered to be lowered as soon as we arrived on the scene. We were going astern but he was holding on. I called to some hands by the torpedo tubes and began to haul him up. Eventually he came over the guard-rail unconscious but still holding on by his hands; his feet had never found the net at all. He was very full of water but we got him for'ard at once and he seemed likely to recover.

About this time too they had an injured man on X gun deck who was got down by Neill Robertson stretcher (the kind in which a man can be strapped for lowering). These stretchers were being used all the time. I went for'ard once to find a petty officer. There was a big crowd outside the Sick Bay and I trod on something in the dark shadow there. It was an injured man and I had tripped over his broken leg. I hope and believe it was still numb enough for him not to be hurt, but it was very distressing to me to feel that I had been so careless. I ought to have known that the congestion of stretchers would be there.

When I was reporting damage to the Captain on one

52

occasion we were just coming alongside so I stayed on the bridge to watch from there, as there was hardly time to get down to the fo'c'sle. The Captain was completely calm. He brought the ship alongside in the same masterly manner as he had already done so often. He was calling the telegraph orders to the Navigating Officer who was passing them to the Coxswain in the wheelhouse. As we ground alongside several jumped. One officer was too late, and grabbed the bottom guard-rail and hung outside the flare, his head and arms only visible to us. There was a great shout from the crowd on *Comorin*'s stern. But we had seen it and already two of our men (Cooke and George) had run forward and were trying to haul the officer on board. The ships rolled and swung together. They would hit exactly where the man dangled over the flare; still the two struggling at the guard-rail could not haul the hanging man to safety. Then as if by magic and with a foot to spare the ships began to roll apart again. But still the man could not be hauled on board; still he hung like a living fender. Again the ships rolled together and again stopped a few inches before he was crushed. As they rolled towards each other for the third time, Cooke and George managed to get a proper hold of the man and he was heaved up to safety and this time the ships crashed together with a rending of metal. The two seamen had never withdrawn even when the impact seemed certain and they had thus saved the officer's life. It was a magnificently brave thing to see.

Another man was not so lucky. In some way at the time of jumping he was crushed between the two ships, and fell at once into the sea as they separated. On the other hand I saw a steward with a cigarette in his mouth and a raincoat over one arm step from one ship to the other, swinging his leg over the guard-rails in a most unhurried manner, just as if he had been stepping across in harbour. It was one of those rare occasions when the rise and fall of the two ships coincided. One man arrived on board riding astride the barrel of 'B' gun and another landed astride the guard-rail. Both were quite unhurt.

After the terrible vibrations set up by the huge waves which broke over the quarter-deck each time that we had to go 'Full astern both', I became anxious about the state of the after compartments.

Actually, of course, all damage was above the water line, although, owing to the rolling and pitching a good deal of water was coming inboard through the numerous rents along the port fo'c'sle flare.

Back on the upper deck we saw a man working at the edge of the fire on the weather side of the *Comorin*'s main deck. We couldn't make out what he was doing, but we discovered afterwards that he was burning the confidential books in the blazing signalmen's mess.

Still we were periodically closing the *Comorin*'s bulging stern, with the wicked-looking rudder and propellers bared from time to time as the massive black shape towered above us. Still the men were jumping as the opportunity arose. Each time there was a chorus from the fo'c'sle of 'Jump! – Jump!'

Although we were keen to persuade as many to jump as possible, I thought it was better to let them judge the time for themselves and told my men not to call out 'jump'.

From one of the survivor officers I discovered there had been two medical officers in *Comorin* – one the ship's doctor, Lt-Commander, RNVR, and another taking passage, a Surgeon Lieutenant, RNVR, but the latter was believed to have gone in one of the boats.

So next time we went in to the *Comorin* I shouted that I wanted the doctor at the next jump if possible, as I knew that our own doctor would be hard pressed with so many casualties. No chance arose that time, but a little later as we closed again I could see the Surgeon Lt-Commander poised on the teak rail waiting to jump. Here was the one man that I really wanted safe but he missed his best opportunity and took the last chance, a jump of twenty feet. He landed beyond the padding, at my feet as I stood on the layer's platform of 'A' gun. He fell flat on his back and lay there quite still. But in a few moments he had come around and ten minutes later, very bruised and stiff, he was at work amongst the injured. He too had barely recovered from 'flu and was quite unused to destroyers; I believe also that he felt very seasick. His work that night was beyond praise.

Casualties were not so heavy now, but there were still a good many owing to the fact that jumpers on the downward plunge of the *Comorin* often met the upward surge of *Broke*'s fo'c'sle. This meant that they were hurled against the deck like a cricket ball against a bat.

We were all soaked through with rain and spray and sweat. It was very hot work in a duffle coat. My arms were still inclined to get cramp if I went up ladders by pulling instead of climbing. However I don't think this interfered with my work at all. I still continued with the wearisome anxious round – fo'c'sle for the jump, assess damage, up to report it, and back to the fo'c'sle for the next jump.

These last jumps were very awkward because the remaining ratings were the less adventurous ones whom it was difficult to persuade to jump. Two of them, senior petty officers, were drunk. They had been pushed over and arrived on board in an incapable condition. I thought they were casualties but was relieved, and at the same time furious to discover they were only incapably drunk. It seemed too much that my stretcher parties should work on two drunken and extremely heavy petty officers, especially as they were the very two on whom the officers in the other ship would be expecting to be able to rely to set a good example to the rest.

Once I sent up to the Captain and suggested that we might perhaps consider rescuing the last few by raft if the damage got any worse, as with well over 100 survivors on board it would be out of proportion to risk losing the ship and all of them to get the last few if there were a good chance of getting those last few in another way. We agreed that we would try this as soon as the damage gave real cause for alarm but not before.

Quite suddenly the number on *Comorin*'s stern seemed to have dwindled. At last we seemed to be in sight of the end. There were about ten, mostly officers. The Captain and Commander were directing from one deck above, with a torch.

At the next jump they all arrived, unhurt, except the Captain and the Commander, who remained to make sure that the ship was clear.

Five minutes later we came in again. The Commander jumped and landed safely. The Captain paused to make sure that he had gone, then jumped too. He caught in a rope which dangled from the deck above, and which turned him round so that he faced his own ship again. At the same moment the *Broke* dropped away and began to roll outwards. The Captain's feet fell outside the guard-rail and it seemed that he must be deflected overboard. But he sat across the wire guard-rail and balanced for a moment before rolling backwards and turning a back somersault on the padding of hammocks. He was quite unhurt, smoking his cigarette, and he had managed to return his monocle so quickly to his eye that I thought he had jumped wearing it.

He turned out to be Captain Hallett – a destroyer Captain of the First War who had served under my father some thirty-five years earlier.

I took him up to the bridge to see my Captain and at forty minutes past midnight we made the signal to *Lincoln*, 'Ship is now clear of all officers and men'.

Rescue operations were now successfully completed. During the past three hours no less than 685 telegraph orders had been passed from the bridge to the engine room and executed without a mistake. Captain Hallet told my Captain that there were still some confidential books in the strong room of the *Comorin* and that he would not feel safe in leaving her until she had sunk. He asked us to torpedo her. Having discussed the possibilities of salvage and decided that they were not practical, we prepared to fire a torpedo. It was fired at rather too great a range and did not hit. Nor did the second or the third. Some time elapsed between these attempts and I went below to examine the situation on the mess decks. 'Anyone here down-hearted?' I asked and received a rousing cheer of 'No'. A lot of water was slopping in through the numerous holes and I started a baling party with buckets. The casualties were mostly in hammocks, some on the lockers and some in the starboard hammock netting. The port side of the mess deck was a shambles. However, since everything seemed to be under control, I went aft to the wardroom and found some thirty-five survivor officers ensconced there. The deck was pretty wet and the red shellac coating had started to come off so that everything soon became stained with red. The flat outside was running with fuel oil and water and baling operations were put in hand.

Then I went back to the bridge and instituted a count of the number of survivors which turned out to be correct and never had to be altered. We had exactly 180 on board. Back in the wardroom I found the Engineer Officer baling away with buckets. He told me that the Gunner had been washed overboard, but had been washed back on board again by the next wave. He was very shaken and had turned in. I discovered also that earlier in the evening when struggling with the manilla, PO Storrs had been pushed over by the rope, but had managed to hold on and be hauled back to safety. At some time or other AB Bates had been washed off the iron deck just by the for'ard funnel and washed back on board again on the quarter deck, a remarkable escape.

As it was now after two a.m. and I had to go on watch at four I tried to get a little sleep in Jeayes's cabin. My own cabin was occupied by a Commissioned Gunner whose arm had been crushed. He had caught hold of the outside of the flag deck. His arm had got between the two ships and been pinched whereupon he had let go and would have fallen into the sea but for the fact that his raincoat was pinched in and held. He hung by it and was hauled in from the flag deck ladder. I afterwards discovered that he had served with my father as an AB in the *Majestic* in 1906 when my father had been Cable Officer in her. He occupied my cabin for the rest of the voyage.

I did not sleep much and I missed the torpedoing of the *Comorin*, which was achieved with either the fourth or fifth torpedo. The sixth had a seized-up stop valve and could not be fired. At 0400 I relieved Jeayes on the bridge. The *Comorin* had not sunk; she was appreciably lower in the water and had a marked list to port instead of the slight one to starboard which she had had during the rescue. The Captain had turned in in the charthouse, but came up for a few minutes. I was on watch by myself and we were patrolling up and down to weather of the blazing wreck until dawn.

By about five-thirty the whole of the after promenade deck of *Comorin* from which the survivors had jumped was ablaze. It was satisfactory to know that we had been justified in attempting the night rescue and that time had been an important factor. At dawn we left *Lincoln* to stand by *Comorin* till she sank and set off home with *Glenartney*.

The return journey entailed a lot of hard work. Baling was continuous for the whole two and a half days. *Glenartney* was ordered to proceed on her journey calling at Freetown to disembark survivors, and we were left alone. The weather worsened and on Monday night we had to reduce speed during the middle watch from eight to six knots owing to the heavy head sea set up by the easterly gale. The water on the mess decks was more than the balers could cope with and was running out over the watertight door sills in waterfalls. There were about sixty tons of water on the upper mess deck – about one foot six inches of water when the ship was on an even keel, and four feet or more when she rolled, with a corresponding cataract when she rolled the other way. Life on the mess decks became very uncomfortable. The forepeak and cable locker were flooded and the fore store was filling. It was an anxious night. But when I came on watch at four a.m. on

Tuesday the gale began to moderate suddenly. One of the survivor officers – an RNR Lieutenant – was keeping watch with me. By five the wind had died away to nothing and an hour later it began to blow from the west. Almost at once the sea began to go down and we were able to increase speed. By noon we were steaming at twenty knots for the Clyde and we arrived there on the morning of Wednesday, 9th April. I spent those two and a half days mainly amongst the survivors for'ard. Lewis and the others were looking after the officers as well as possible in the wardroom. The for'ard mess deck seemed to need most of my efforts, and besides I enjoyed the company of the rating survivors, so I spent as much time as I could on the mess deck amongst them. The *Comorin*'s Commander co-operated most kindly by providing three watches of baling parties with two officers in charge of each watch and by helping with other work. Three survivor officers shared the night watches with us on the bridge.

In spite of the apparently heavy casualties during the rescue, so many of these recovered quickly that there were finally only about twenty–five hospital cases out of the whole 180.

We arrived at Greenock at about ten-thirty in the morning and were alongside for rather less than one hour before slipping and proceeding to Londonderry. During that hour the hospital cases were taken into the ambulances, the remainder were put into buses, the two POs who had been drunk on the Sunday night and had been under open arrest ever since were taken away under escort from HMS *Hecla*, and our bread and meat that we had ordered by signal were embarked. I went ashore to give parting encouragement to the injured in the ambulance, and met an old school friend, David Colville, Lt RNVR. That same evening we were back at our base in Londonderry.

To complete the story – we learned that the fire in *Comorin* was an accident. A broken oil pipe at the top of the boiler room had dripped hot oil on a Stoker and made him drop a torch which had ignited the oil on the deck. In a flash the boiler room was blazing and had to be closed down at once. This meant that there was no power on the fire main and therefore nothing with which to fight the fire.

Lincoln came into Londonderry two days later and told us of the sinking of *Comorin*. They had fired sixty-three rounds and two torpedos at her. The torpedos – not supposed to be fired at all being American pattern – had not hit. They did not reckon at first that their shells did much good. But as the fore hatch cover was near the water, owing to her pronounced list they pounded this and made a hole there large enough to flood the forehold. One of the motor-boats floated off undamaged. Then the ship heeled over and finally the stern came right out of the water and she plunged down. She had sunk by about noon Monday, 7th April. *Lincoln* had saved 121, *Glenartney* about 109. *Lincoln* had most of the army survivors one of whom had been crushed between boat and destroyer.

Just after leaving Greenock for the Foyle we received the following signal from the Flag Officer in Charge, Greenock:

'I have heard with great pleasure of your oustanding display of seamanship in rescuing survivors and send you and your ship's company warm congratulations. I am proud that my old ship should have done so well. 1245/9.'

And on the following day we received this signal:

'To *Broke*, Repeated C-in-C, Western Approaches, FOIC, Greenock, From Admiralty and First Sea Lord personally: Congratulations on the fine seamanship you displayed in going repeatedly alongside *Comorin* in heavy weather. 0400/10.'

After the *Comorin* adventure *Broke* was once more back in the dockyard at Belfast.

Leslie Thomas

AUTHOR

In the 1960s I was voyaging among the islands, then called The New Hebrides, in the South Pacific. I was told that on one lofty island there was a radio station and, being anxious to learn if my football team, Queens Park Rangers, had reached the Final of the League Cup in far-off England, I took a small boat to the island.

Let no one say that the Pacific is pacific – because it isn't! After a terrible trip we eventually arrived off the island, where I had to swim ashore and then clamber up a hill of mud and tangled growth. Exhausted, dirty, bleeding, I reached the top and staggered into the wireless station. A lone, fat, white man in a pair of old shorts was there in charge of half a dozen natives.

As Britishers do, we formally introduced ourselves but he became less amiable when I asked about the Queens Park Rangers football result.

'I dunno, mate' he said. 'I'm a Millwall supporter.'

John Schlesinger CBE

FILM DIRECTOR

My first trip across the Atlantic was from New York to Southampton on the *Queen Elizabeth* in the mid-sixties.

I was travelling alone and, on the first night out at dinner, I asked the Chief Steward to place me at an entertaining table. He assured me that the ship's Doctor was the most amusing member of the crew, and thus I found myself at his table, sandwiched between a lady from the New York Cunard offices, and a librarian from the North of England who talked, or rather sang, to himself throughout the five days were were at sea – and this included the menu for every meal. It was a new experience to hear a musical version of consommé madriléne and saumon poché with hollandaise sauce. Also at the table was another lady from the Cunard offices and the other four places were unoccupied.

In the middle of our meal we were joined by three late arrivals – a lawyer from Boston, his wife and daughter but no ship's Doctor. The lawyer was a rather burly man with an affable personality and, having introduced himself and his family to our table, he sat down, rubbed his hands together and decided it was time to order a drink. His wife leaned across to him, there was a hastily-whispered conversation and he ordered a club soda.

It was clear that there was some bone of contention between them, and before long the poor man started to have a fit, which turned out to be withdrawal symptoms from alcoholism. No sign of the Doctor, and the librarian continued to sing to himself louder than ever. The two Cunard ladies quoted the lyrics from *Do I Hear A Waltz*, which was a current Broadway hit, and the Bostonian's daughter, who had buck teeth, said, 'He's never been this bad'.

It occurred to me that medical help was needed, so I left the table and telephoned the ship's hospital, only to be told that they would send an orderly as quickly as possible but they were extremely busy. When I returned to the table the unfortunate man had been laid out on the floor, and the children at the next table were being told to 'Turn around and get on with your dinner'.

The ship's Doctor did not appear until the third night out at sea.

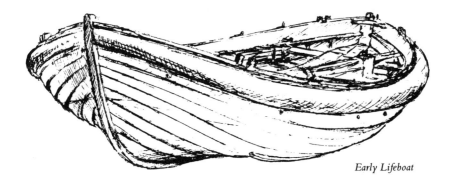

Early Lifeboat

Richard Baker
Lt Cdr (Retd) OBE RD

BROADCASTER AND AUTHOR

During the war, when I was a Midshipman RNVR, I served in the sloop HMS *Peacock* which was sent to do its working-up training at Tobermory on the Isle of Mull. In charge there was the legendary 'Monkey' Stephenson, Vice-Admiral Sir Gilbert Stephenson – known by many nicknames, among them 'The Terror of Tobermory'.

He was a fearsome old gentlemen, whatever your rank, and midshipmen – particularly RNVR midshipmen – were less than the dust. On my 19th birthday a great party took place in the wardroom of *Peacock*, which was extravagantly enjoyed by all. Towards midnight, I thought it would be amusing to set off a fire extinguisher, and covered myself in foam.

'I say', said the Doctor, 'do you know that's dangerous acid?' Believing him, I followed to the Sick Bay where he gave me two huge tablets of gentian violet ointment and told me to rub it well in, especially on any exposed parts. Having dutifully obeyed, I retired for the night, too 'tired and emotional' to realise what I'd done.

The full horror dawned next morning. The whole of my face was bright mauve, exactly the colour of a RNVR midshipman's lapel tabs. Nothing would shift the dye, and I was not much consoled when the Doctor told me breezily that it would wear off in about a fortnight.

The Captain was vastly amused at the thought of having the Navy's only mauve midshipman and cruelly decided to show me off to the Admiral. I was despatched to his flagship with some message. After listening to what I had to say with a more or less straight face , the Admiral asked, 'And what is your job on board, sonny?'

64

'I'm assistant Gunnery Officer, sir', I said, 'and Sports and Entertainments Officer.'

'Oh', was the reply. 'I see you take the second part of your job VERY seriously.

The Rt Hon Lord Shackleton
KG PC OBE

In September 1934, as a member of the Oxford University Ellesmere Land Expedition, I was engaged with one companion in laying depots up the North-West coast of Greenland for use on the sledge journeys which we planned for the Spring. We were in a small dory with an outboard motor when we were caught in new ice. Sea water ice, as it begins to freeze, is rather like glue. Later it becomes rubbery. We were unable to get the boat free, and, in the end, pulled it up on to an ice floe.

We had not expected to be out for more than a couple of days, and therefore had little in the way of equipment and no sleeping bags, but luckily we did have a tent and a primus which worked very effectively. That was a cold and miserable night. The following morning we found that our floe was caught up with the rest of the pack ice, and we were drifting rapidly out to sea. Next stop Baffin Island, some hundreds of miles distant. We tried to pull the boat over the new ice, but it was not strong enough, and I went through. We clambered back on to the floe and my companion took off half his clothes and gave them to me – the quickest change I have ever made in my life! And so we drifted. Then, as we thought to make matters worse, a storm blew up, but in fact this was what saved us, for it broke up the ice. We were then about eight miles from land and we had a very anxious crossing. Indeed, it was so scaring that for the first time in my life in a rough sea I did not feel sea-sick! As we neared land, the propeller hit some ice, and that knocked the outboard out, but we were close enough by then to row to the shore.

I do not necessarily recommend this as a cure for sea-sickness, but it was not the last time I found a near disaster solving the problem.

Coming home from Greenland the following year, the propeller on our schooner, which had obviously been damaged in ice, fell-off, and the fact that we had to rely on sail cured my sea-sickness! We finally beached our ship in Castlebay, Barra.

Major S E Southby-Tailyour
OBE

ROYAL MARINES

During Operation Corporate, we had been in San Carlos for a
week or so and suffered the worst the Argentinian Air Force
could throw at us – and yet were still unblasé about airstrikes.
Thus, each time we heard a whistle blow, or the ships in San
Carlos blow their sirens, we dived for cover into the nearest
slit trench.

One morning, shortly after the Army's 5th Brigade had
arrived, we seemed to be having more than the usual number
of air raids. On the umpteenth time of diving into a water-
filled trench on a whistle blast, we looked up over the parapet
to watch for enemy aircraft, only to see a newly-arrived Army
detachment playing soccer on the Settlement's 'village green'.

Every time there was a 'foul' we older hands went to Air
Raid Warning Red! Although we saw the funny side, it was
the last football match to be played before the Argentinian
surrender.

Sir Michael Hordern CBE

ACTOR

I can't remember now whether I fell or whether I was pushed when, in the summer of 1940, as an ordinary seaman in training at Plymouth Barracks, I volunteered for service in DEMS (Defensively Equipped Merchant Ships) fondly known as 'Dems'. After rudimentary gunnery training I was drafted to the good ship *City of Florence* loading at Newport with high explosive – mostly 15" shells for the battleships of the British Fleet in Alexandria.

Our armament consisted of an ancient First War 4" gun (anti-submarine) and a veteran 12-pounder (anti-aircraft) and the guns' crew of press-ganged Merchant Seamen was cajoled into some sort of shape by a retired corporal of the Royal Marines and myself – now exalted to Acting Able-Seaman gunlayer.

A fire broke out on board while we were loading and all the high explosive was unloaded again. Hooray, we thought, they'll now replace high explosive with cotton-wool or timber or something friendly but no, they put all those projectiles back again and we sailed.

Off Liverpool we joined our convoy, some 15–20 merchantmen escorted by two armed trawlers. The following evening, my second day at sea ever, a lovely September dusk, off the N. Ireland island of Innistrahull – the name is engraved on my heart – we were attacked by a U-boat 'Wolf Pack' and the five ships nearest to us went down in ten minutes. It concentrates the mind wonderfully to be attacked by U-boats as you sit on top of ten thousand tons of T.N.T. We loaded our 4" and swung it this way and that but never saw so much as a periscope.

In those early days, convoy discipline was somewhat loose, the ships sounding off and stumbling over each other like a

68

flock of sheep trying to get through a gap in a hedge. Came the dawn we found ourselves quite alone on the wide Atlantic, our gun still loaded.

The shell had jammed in the breach but the skipper, fearful that the Germans might hear us, wouldn't allow us to shoot it out. It wasn't until six weeks later in the peace of the Indian Ocean, with the shell properly rusted in, that he gave the word and we pulled the trigger – but that's another story.

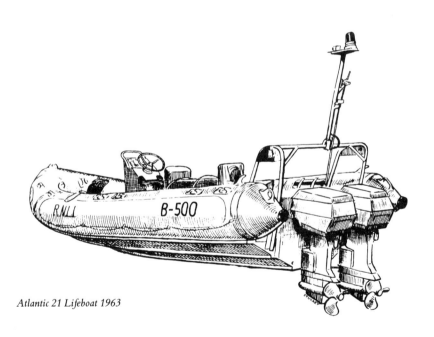

Atlantic 21 Lifeboat 1963

Commander David Cobb
CVO RN DL

DEPUTY DIRECTOR OF THE
DUKE OF EDINBURGH'S AWARD SCHEME

In a tribute to the late Lt Colonel James Myatt CVO, Chief Executive of the Royal Bath and West Show, Commander Cobb spoke at a Thanksgiving Service in Wells Cathedral of his 'extensive work for sail training with many different organisations and with young people from many different backgrounds, some under-privileged, starting in the early '60s with participation in the Tall Ships Races.

'It was at the end of the 1962 race that the STA announced the next race in two years' time was to be Transatlantic. James immediately volunteered to raise an entry, an idea that seemed an impossibility to those associated with him, but, quite undeterred by the pessimists, he proceeded to scour the coasts and registers for a suitable vessel for such an ambitious venture. Hardly anyone thought he would succeed and after a year of trying it really did seem as if he wouldn't when, in the winter of 1963, he spied a most beautiful 50 ton yawl, gleaming green enamel and gold finish, refitting at Plymouth.

'Finding that the owners lived nearby, he rang up from a call box to make what many would think a preposterous proposition – could he borrow her to sail to New York with a crew of inexperienced youngsters? Surprisingly, he was not rebuffed, but invited to meet them the next day when, after listening to James' most persuasive proposals, they very generously agreed to the idea.

'With their support and kindness, James' dream became a reality, and *Tawau*, as she was called, became the successful British entry in that race. It was only some months after his meeting with the owners that James found they only agreed to discuss the suggestion at all because, through some indistinctness in his voice on the 'phone, they mistook him for a friend of theirs – Sir Miles Wyatt, himself a distinguished yachtsman.'

Stanley Nelson

DESIGNER

I am indebted to my great friend Ronald Dyer, owner and skipper of the ketch *Eugene Marie* for indulging my love of boats and the sea by allowing my wife and me to crew for him quite regularly.

After a few days' coastal sailing, we felt the need for dinner ashore, so we put into Plymouth Sound and on up to Spaniards where there is a good inn with private moorings. After an excellent meal we turned in, having planned an early start next morning.

With the motor idling and self at the helm, Ron cast off at the bow. Perhaps it was the early hour, but in a moment of aberration, instead of drifting back from the buoy, I drove over it.

Silently the line wound itself round the propeller shaft, followed by an ominous thunk as the pick-up buoy smacked into the screw and the motor ground to a stop.

So we put a dinghy over the side and tied a line round Ron's waist, and he went straight over into the murky water, knife in hand, hoping to cut the line from the propellor shaft. He made several unavailing attempts to cut it free.

It was then decided that, as I had committed the offence, I should take the dinghy ashore to get help. We were only 50 yards out, so I was soon climbing up the steps to the inn, where stood the landlord.

I said to him, 'I'm afraid I've got into trouble and have driven over your moorings'. He said, 'I know, we have been watching you, but don't worry, a lot of idiots do that up here'.

He said we would be needing a diver. Fortunately he knew of one, a regular customer who usually came in for his lunchtime pint about 12 o'clock. A quick phone call by the landlord to the diver's mother confirmed that he would be in today. So back in the dinghy to the ketch with the good news.

By 11.45 we were in the bar with G. and T.s waiting for the diver to show up, (we found he was a professional diver who worked at the dockyard down the Sound).

Suddenly the landlord, who was looking out of the window, said, 'Here he comes now'.

In walked the diver – with his right arm in plaster. He had just broken it.

But there was a happy ending to this sad story. The diver got in touch with a friend who turned up to help us – a friend who refused the offer of the dinghy out to the ketch, preferring to swim out in trunks and mask. He called up for a sharp knife, and promptly cut us loose. And when it was over, he swam ashore again.

Mike Yarwood OBE

ENTERTAINER

Margaret Thatcher fell off Brighton Pier into the sea. She was just about to drown when Arthur Scargill, who was taking a stroll on the water, spotted her.

'Hang on Maggie, I'll save you', shouted Arthur. He dragged Maggie on to the beach to safety.

'Thank you Arthur, you saved my life. Is there anything I can do to repay you?'

'Well', said Arthur, 'There is one thing I would like.'

'Yes, what is it?' asked Maggie.

'I would like a State Funeral', said Arthur.

'That's an odd request', said Maggie. 'Why do you want a State Funeral?'

'Well', said Arthur, 'When my members find out I've saved your life – they'll kill me.'

Harry Radford

EX-MERCHANT MARINE CHIEF RADIO OPERATOR

I first went to sea as a 'sparks' in the First World War, not on glamorous liners but tramp steamers. On one Atlantic crossing from Southampton, for instance, I remember we were passed five times by the crack liner of the day, the *Mauretania*. Twice we sighted her, three more times I picked her up by radio as she passed while we continued to make our 8–12 knots crossing to New York.

Once during that first war I had the experience of taking to the boats when we ran aground in the St Lawrence river and were ordered to abandon ship, but this did not really prepare me for the second occasion when I had to take to the boats with fellow crew members in the Second World War.

Our ship, the *Statira,* had taken on a cargo of manganese ore and manganese rods in India. It was 1941 and the cargo was so valuable to the war effort that we went round the Cape to avoid the risk of going through the Mediterranean. We got as far as the North coast of Scotland, via Belfast.

We were in a convoy of about 14 or 15 ships, when, on a fine summer's night, we were attacked by German bombers. The first I knew of it was at 2.00 a.m. when two explosions threw me out of my bunk.

The *Statira* had been hit by at least two bombs and was quickly listing and was on fire. We were told to take to the boats and abandon ship. We were armed with an anti-aircraft gun and the gunner who joined us at Belfast didn't look any more than a schoolboy. Soon everybody was off the ship except him. He was firing at the German aeroplanes and they were firing their guns at us in the life-boats. It was a ghastly experience, I have never been so frightened in my life. When you are in a small boat and someone is firing at you, you put your head down and try to curl up into as small a ball as possible.

Our young gunner had plenty of guts and kept firing at the aeroplanes but the rest of the crew waiting for him in the lifeboats started shouting 'Stop firing you silly little bugger and come on'. Eventually he came off the ship and down into the boats, but I must admit he did his job.

We had the most important cargo of any of the ships in the convoy and we were the only ship of any size to be sunk. I don't know if they really came after us or whether it was just chance.

The sea was calm and it was a lovely night but most of the crew were wearing only underwear. I was lucky. As I left my cabin I grabbed coats which were hanging on the back of my door.

Eventually we were picked up from our lifeboats by two Tribal Class destroyers which came looking for us. They put ladders down the sides and we went aboard for a thrilling ride to Stornaway on the Isle of Lewis. Our only casualty had been one man with wet feet.

Dawn was breaking as we got in, but our arrival was not to go unnoticed. Customs officers were waiting on the quay and as our dishevelled crew stepped onto the quay, (for the most part wearing the only belongings they had managed to save from the lost ship), the Customs asked us if we had anything to declare.

They got some right answers.

Donald Sinden CBE

ACTOR AND AUTHOR

In his autobiography *A Touch of the Memoirs* Donald Sinden recalls the filming of *The Cruel Sea*:

The ship's captain was required to take the ship out to sea and out of sight of land because all the scenes due to be filmed were exteriors (the interiors could be done later in the studio). The 'quality' of light has to be consistent throughout and many hours were spent waiting for clouds to pass (as Cedric Hardwicke once said, 'Filming is ninety-five per cent boredom, five per cent panic'). Then suddenly the captain and his crew had to produce 'Full steam ahead'.

Now if a duologue were to be shot the sun was expected to maintain its position on an actor's face for several minutes. This required an extremely accurate course to be steered. Once the shot on one actor was completed, the whole ship had to be turned around to produce equivalent light on actor number two. This operation can take some time. The ship is then required to steer an equally accurate course in the reverse direction.

One day some colleagues and I were keeping out of sight by hiding in the wheelhouse while a scene not involving us was filmed on the bridge. The coxswain was a large, florid, clean-shaven man with an apparent ability to forestall and pre-empt his captain's orders.

He regaled us with splendid anecdotes of his life in the Navy. Halfway through a sentence the captain's voice echoed down the voice pipe, 'Starboard fifteen'. Before the word had been completed the coxswain was already spinning his wheel as he repeated, 'Starboard fifteen – fifteen of starboard wheel on, sir'; he then completed the anecdote with no pause for breath. We all continued to chat away, each anecdote engendering another as the ship's engines thundered away at Full Speed Ahead. Some time later we were interrupted by the captain, screaming dementedly down the voice pipe, 'WHAT COURSE ARE YOU STEERING?!' Quite unperturbed and in the calmest of voice, the coxswain replied, '360° for the fourth time round, sir'.

His was not to reason why.

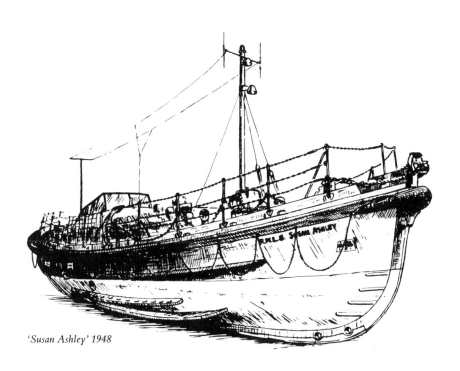

'Susan Ashley' 1948

Richard Pasco CBE

ACTOR

'You'll be home for Christmas, mate, so don't worry.'

'Oh yes?' I sighed with disbelief, but the fact was that Demob group 63, having spent the last year of its army service with the Forces Broadcasting Services, Jerusalem (those who belonged to that group in that particular area at that time, early December 1947), were filled with anxious and enjoyable trepidation that their three-and-a-half-year gaol sentence in H.M. Army was, indeed, about to come to an end. After a hilarious ten days in Port Said transit camp – awaiting a ship to take us on to Liverpool or Tilbury or anywhere that was *England* – we eventually embarked on the ex-Cunard liner ss *Samaria* sometime towards the end of December (Christmas under canvas in the sand – in true army fashion!). The ship was packed from stem to stern with all kinds of troops from the Far East and on her arrival in Port Said to pick *us* up, we wondered, exactly, where we could fit in. I 'fitted in' somewhere in the bowels of the ship slung in a hammock next to the ship's refrigerator where the icy blast and stench of freezing meats etc., overpowered us every time the door was opened. Then – the *pièce de resistance* of the whole voyage – the Bay of Biscay in early January. . . ! Sea sickness en masse; the decks were awash with what can only be described as 'vomit' and all feelings of a happy release from the army service were abandoned! *Anything* to get off that bucking bronco of a boat (sorry, ship!).

We arrived in Liverpool ten days after leaving Port Said sometime in the middle of January – HOME BY CHRISTMAS!? – Green, weak, ill, determined never again to go to sea – *swim* in it, *look* at it, *read* about it but at all costs go *on* it – ever again!

All this, too, happening to someone who is *supposed* to be related to Lord Nelson's Flag Officer, John Pasco! Ashamed of myself – ? Frankly, no, I remain convinced that seasickness is the worst *minor* illness and the least pleasant sensation available to mankind!

Barbara Cartland D St J

AUTHORESS AND PLAYWRIGHT

I never laugh at people being frightened either in the air, or at sea.

I believe it is because Lady Diana Cooper was frightened that I am alive today. In 1924 we were in a yacht, the *Mairi,* going to Deauville and ran into very bad weather. Lady Diana insisted on turning round in mid-Channel and returning to Southampton.

Our party travelled on the ordinary cross-Channel steamer and the yacht went off without us, but two yachts were wrecked in the storm that night.

Had the *Mairi,* which was owned by Lord Birkenhead the famous KC and was never very seaworthy, had another six people on board, she might easily have capsized.

In a cloakroom of the fashionable Embassy Club, I met Lady Diana whom I had not seen since our trip to Deauville several years earlier.

I approached her shyly because she always seemed to me like a goddess, far removed from mere mortals like myself and said: 'I must thank you, Lady Diana, for saving my life. If you had not turned the yacht round that time we were going to Deauville, I am certain it would have gone to the bottom and we should all have been drowned.'

'I was glad to save my own life', she answered, her blue eyes almost as translucent as the mirror which reflected them, her hair golden as pale corn, her face that of a saint.

'Did you know', I asked, 'that the yacht took three days to reach Trouville harbour and that everything on board was smashed?'

'How thankful I am that we turned back!' Lady Diana murmured.

A story is told that once in a storm Lady Diana went on her knees to the Captain of the *Majestic* en route for New York and asked him to turn back, but he refused!

I loathe the sea. On another occasion the yacht I was in, which had been chartered by the Cunningham-Reids, was nearly wrecked off the Balearic Islands. The portholes burst open, I lay soaked on my bunk and was too sick to care.

When we reached harbour and asked for a cup of tea, the only piece of china on board which wasn't broken was a sauceboat!

This excerpt is from I Search for Rainbows *by Barbara Cartland.*

Major S E Southby-Tailyour
OBE

ROYAL MARINES

Roger and I were sailing in the Two-Handed Round Britain and Ireland Race in a beautiful 50-foot yawl and were becalmed somewhere North of the Scillies when a pigeon landed on board. There was not a breath of wind and the yacht was rolling gently in the long swell. After three days of no movement the pigeon moved below and sat on the VHF set which was at the head of the chart table. It faced forward with its tail perched over that part of the chart that covered the approaches to Cork Harbour. Although it had steadfastly refused to eat, this had made no difference to its other bodily functions! Cork was, therefore, more easy to find from the upper deck in the heat haze than from the chart.

This state of affairs lasted another day or so during which time we became decidedly bored with the pigeon but too superstitious to take any positive action. Roger was below, off watch, lying stark naked on his back in the starboard pilot berth up under the starboard deck head. He now knows that this was his first mistake.

For some unexplained reason, the pigeon suddenly decided to take a little violent exercise. I was so astounded at this sudden and unexpected activity after so long, that I rushed from the wheel to the companion hatch to watch. This was another mistake as I was then blocking its only escape avenue.

The pigeon panicked and began flapping its wings in short jerky movements as it fluttered round the cabin looking for somewhere to land. Deep in its simple brain it knew that it had to look for a branch or twig (or bough, depending on how you view these things) and so it was with an obvious sense of relief that it landed on that part of Roger's body that most closely resembled an acceptable landing site.

Roger shot bolt upright (or nearly so for he hit his head very hard on the deck head) and took stock of the situation. Without further thought, he made his second mistake. With the back of his hand, he swept the pigeon from its roost; unfortunately it was holding on with all its might (and six claws) to keep a balance in the long Atlantic swell.

The pigeon left the yacht immediately, but the scars (I am told) exist to this day.

Captain John Coote RN

SUBMARINE SPECIALIST AND EDITOR
'SHELL PILOT TO THE SOUTH COAST HARBOURS'

Trebetherick in the endless summer of 1946 was perfect for an extended leave. As a change from losing precious Dunlop '65s in rabbit warrens on the golf-course, I used to go out in an open workboat with the mechanic of the Padstow life-boat, a great character with fingers like leather bananas. Sometimes we plundered a small island off Rumps Head for gulls' eggs. Always we hauled up his lobster-pots, locating their half-submerged floats from secret transits on shore.

The evenings were spent consuming some of the catch in

the back room of the pub at Rock and acquiring a taste for scrumpy and hand-bell ringing. On my last day, sweating to pull a pot in deep water, I told my friend to be in precisely the same spot at 1100 hours in a week's time, with a bag of lobsters ready for transfer.

I went back to Rothesay, whence we sailed down the Irish Sea. Off Tintagel we dived for trim and headed for the rendezvous outside Padstow. Sure enough, there was the boat, soon filling the periscope with her owner looking at his watch and gazing out to seaward. Right alongside him we blew everything and surfaced as though for gun action. A heaving-line from the casing sent over a bottle of Scotch and half jar of pussar's rum. Back came a bulging, dripping sack.

Within two minutes we had dived, resumed course for Hongkong and the chef was popping lobsters into boiling water to feed most of the ship's company.

I am told that, to his dying day this summer, Bill Orchard kept his secret rendezvous with HM Submarine *Amphion* to himself. I hope the local life-boat crew scattered his ashes right on the spot, preferably in an empty rum jar.

Footnote: Bill Orchard was mechanic on the Padstow life-boats from 1931 until he retired through ill health in 1949. He died in May 1983 at the age of 79. His ashes were scattered from the Padstow lifeboat over his old fishing grounds.

Clare Francis OBE

SINGLE-HANDED YACHTSWOMAN
TELEVISION PRESENTER AND WRITER

For me, it's never the storms and the gales which cast terror into my heart, it's the *solid* things – like land, icebergs, or shingle banks. And with good reason. On the 1976 Transatlantic Singlehanded Race I woke up to find I had sailed between two rather large icebergs. I didn't need to be told how lucky I had been – my knocking knees informed me. I sat down rather suddenly and gave myself a brandy.

Then there was the volcano which wasn't meant to be there. It popped up out of the blue and gave me a terrible shock. It was on my first solo Atlantic crossing in 1973 and, needless to say, I had made an error in my navigation. Not surprising really – I had taught myself from a book and this was my first chance to put the theory into practice. Anyway, the volcano was quite harmless – Terciera, one of the Azores Group – and it was still many miles away. But it *looked* very close, silhouetted black against the evening sky. I still shudder at the memory!

But the worst occasion was the time when I nearly stranded my boat on a sandbank – right outside my home port. Again, it was very early in my big-boat sailing career. I was taking *Gulliver G* out through Hurst Narrows at the Western end of the Solent when, anxious to identify every single buoy correctly, I went below to the chart table. I was only there for a minute, but it was long enough for the tide to sweep *Gulliver G* sideways onto the Shingles Bank. Crash! Her keel dropped onto the bank with a terrible thud and the whole boat shuddered. I could almost hear her thinking: What idiot's in charge here? Fortunately the story had a happy ending. A wave lifted the boat clear again and she sailed to safety.

I certainly learnt a lesson that day – learn your buoys *before* you set out and navigate by the tried and true eyeball!

Whenever I sail past the Shingles nowadays, I still breathe a sigh of relief, not just because I got away without damaging my boat, but because I didn't have to call out the life-boat.

For any proud and independent British sailor, that would be the *worst thing that could happen at sea!*

Denis Norden CBE

SCRIPTWRITER AND BROADCASTER

I'm afraid I have no sea-going anecdote for your book – much as I'd like to help – because I've suffered all my life from an inordinate and unreasonable fear of anything to do with being upon the waters. I believe the medical name for this condition is 'ship-scared'.

ABSON BOOKS

RHYMING COCKNEY SLANG – 85p. A glossary to help you use your loaf (of bread – head) in getting about London.

AMERICAN ENGLISH – 85p. A glossary of everyday words which have completely different meanings depending upon which side of the Atlantic you happen to be.

SCOTTISH ENGLISH – 85p. A glossary of everyday Scottish words. Informative for newcomers and visitors – evocative for expatriates.

IRISH ENGLISH – 85p. A glossary of words to help disentangle the Irish gift of the gab.

AUSTRALIAN ENGLISH – 85p. A glossary of words which are helpful to all who journey to or from the world's largest island and smallest continent.

GET SQUASH STRAIGHT, or it's even more fun when you win – £1.25 by Derek Robinson. Telling tactics which almost certainly guarantee the overthrow of your opponent.

CITY OF LONDON SAFARI – £1.95 by Helen Long. A charming lion lives at St. Paul's Cathedral. He is just one of the many creatures, including dragons, cats, grasshoppers and beavers who have taken up residence in the square mile of the City of London. All can be searched out and seen free with the help of this book.

A GALLIMAUFRY OF SUPERSTITIONS AND OLD WIVES' TALES – £1.25 by Hilary Cannock. A fascinating collection of superstitions gathered from all over the British Isles.

 All available from booksellers or by adding 15p for the first copy and 8p per copy thereafter for packing and postage from the publishers, Abson Books, Abson, Wick, Bristol BS15 5TT, England.